The North Wales Limestone Way

Colin K. Peter

Gwasg Carreg Gwalch

First published in 2023
© text & photos: Colin K. Peter

All rights reserved. No part of this publication may be reproduced, stored in a retrieval system, or transmitted in any form or by any means, electronic, electrostatic, magnetic tape, mechanical, photocopying, recording, or otherwise, without prior permission of the authors of the works herein.

ISBN: 978-1-84524-460-6
Cover design: Eleri Owen

Published by Gwasg Carreg Gwalch,
12 Iard yr Orsaf, Llanrwst, Wales LL26 0EH
tel: 01492 642031
email: books@carreg-gwalch.cymru
website: www.carreg-gwalch.cymru

Pen y Corddyn Mawr Hillfort and cliffs from across the Dulas Valley

Contents

INTRODUCTION — 4
  The Route
  Stages
  Accommodation
  Transport
  Tourist information centres
  Refreshments
  Maps
  Waymarking
  SSSIs, SACs and nature reserves
  Data Sources

STAGE 1: Llandudno, Great Orme to Rhos on Sea — 12

STAGE 2: Rhos on Sea to Abergele — 27

STAGE 3: Abergele to Denbigh — 41

STAGE 4: Denbigh to Llanfair Dyffryn Clwyd — 58

STAGE 5: Llanfair Dyffryn Clwyd to Maeshafn — 73

STAGE 6: Maeshafn to Brynford — 90

STAGE 7: Brynford to Prestatyn — 108

APPENDICES
Appendix 1:
  Glossary of Welsh Place Names — 129
Appendix 2:
  SSSIs, SACs and Nature Reserves — 131
Appendix 3:
  Further Reading — 132

Introduction

The North Wales Limestone Way is a newly-created 136km (85 mile) seven-stage route along the outcrop of the 340–330 million year old Carboniferous Limestone from the iconic Great Orme in Llandudno along the North Wales coast and around the Vale of Clwyd, crossing the Clwydian Hills via a low pass to the Northeast Wales limestone uplands to finish on the coast at Prestatyn. The route starts and ends in popular Victorian seaside resorts, but in between moves inland to much quieter places. It covers a wealth of history and pre-history passing Stone Age cave dwellings, Bronze Age copper mines, Iron Age hillforts, Roman ruins, Norman castles and walled towns, historic houses and remnants of the industrial past through to modern Wales with offshore wind farms and oil/gas platforms.

Coastal and inland scenery is stunning with nature reserves and their specialised floras widespread. The limestone gives good walking, usually dry underfoot, with a scattering of limestone villages; drystone walls often defining the fields, and woodlands carpeted with spring flowers.

The walk closely follows the outcrop of the Carboniferous Limestone (363–290Ma), but locally strays onto older or younger rocks. Most of North Wales from the Conwy Valley to the Cheshire Plain is floored by grey Silurian mudstones and sandstones that accumulated in a deep sea. These are readily apparent when the walk crosses the uplifted Clwydian Hills and locally along the much-faulted western side of the Vale of Clwyd.

Elsewhere Silurian outcrops are scarce.

To the west of the Vale of Clwyd, reddish purple mudstones and sandstones, in a belt about 1km wide, form the earliest Carboniferous sediments; they sit on the Silurian land surface (the Wales-London-Brabant Massif). They are seldom exposed, but give a rich red-purple colour to the derived soil.

The Carboniferous Limestones themselves, light grey-brown, but weathering creamy white, were deposited in clear, tropical, shallow water with fossils such as corals, shells and crinoids (sea lilies) often visible. North of the present-day coastline, via a patchy reef belt, deeper marine conditions prevailed.

The Carboniferous Limestone is succeeded by Millstone Grit sandstones and then the rocks of the Coal Measures. These are not often seen on the walk; they lie further east (North Wales Coalfield) and underlie Prestatyn, although Gloddaeth Purple Sandstones seen on Stage 1 are believed to be of this age.

In the Vale of Clwyd, a down-faulted rift, Triassic rocks (245–208Ma) are characterised by desert sediments, typically red dune sandstones, with the intervening rugged hills being the source of sediment. These sediments are rarely seen at the surface, but on this walk near Ruthin, an excellent road cutting and buildings display the bright red sandstone.

In the Pleistocene, from around 300,000 until 10,000 years ago, most of Great Britain was affected by three glacial and succeeding inter-glacial periods and many of the soils we see today are glacial till. The highlands of North Wales were intermittently covered by up to a kilometre of ice and the landscapes we see are a result of the action of glaciers as they carved out valleys then, as they retreated, left glacial landforms, erratics and sediments. The Vale of Clwyd reveals evidence of ice streams from the North Wales highlands to the west, but also from an Irish Sea Ice flow coming down from the north – and reaching as far south as Denbigh. Evidence indicates that the southern part of the Vale of Clwyd was intermittently the site of a large lake. In the interglacial periods the area was a site of early human habitation.

The scenery, however, is to an extent also controlled by geological faults with a more ancient history and which even today act as the location of earthquakes. Amongst the most important are the NE/SW Menai Straits Fault Zone, the N/S Vale of Clwyd and Alyn Valley Faults, and the NE/SW Aber Dinlle Fault which runs through Llandudno, separating the Great and Little Ormes. In the west Vale of Clwyd several N/S faults chop up the exposures of Carboniferous Limestone. The Llanelidan Fault, running east-west, terminates the limestone outcrops in the west of the Vale of Clwyd and effectively forms the southern end of the Clwydian Hills.

Comments on the geology encountered are given in the stage descriptions, with appropriate photographs.

The Route

From Llandudno you could take the Number 13 bus to Prestatyn, taking 45 minutes; alternatively spend a more interesting seven days walking the long way round!

Whilst never ascending above 400 metres, the route often has superb scenery and coastal views. It uses public footpaths, bridleways, open-access land and some minor roads over undulating hills and quiet valleys with occasional steep ascents and descents. Except for Llandudno, very few of the footpaths are well used; occasional dog walkers, farmers and rare walkers may be encountered. Many will be happy to pass the time of day with you and discuss the weather and your plans.

Limestone often offers ideal walking country; the soils are often thin and free-draining, the rocks are commonly resistant to weathering and so occupy higher ground with consequent wide-ranging views, and because of limited agricultural use and ancient mining the land is often well-wooded or left as open-access land. In addition limestone soils often reward us with specialised flora – wild flowers are widespread and nature reserves and SSSIs (Sites of Special Scientific Investigation) are frequently encountered.

Three things to be wary of; when limestone is polished by heavy foot traffic it becomes very slippery when wet. In woods, typically with shallow soils, tree roots are often on the surface and may be a trip hazard on paths. You will doubtless come across electric fences across the path in some of the fields; there is often an insulated spring-clip to use as a gate, or you may have to stride over, or roll under them. Always assume they are live!

Stages

The seven stages as described range from 10.8 to 13.6 miles (17.3 to 21.8km) with total daily ascent from 1345 to 2320 ft. (410 to 707m). Stages are designed to provide accommodation at the end of each day; where accommodation is scarce it may be easier to have bases in the larger towns for two to three days and use the local buses to reach the beginning or end of the stage. Each stage also has a section on how best to complete the stage as a day trip. Welsh residents over 60 can use their bus passes for free travel; Other UK bus passes are not usually valid in Wales. Facilities, including toilets, are sometimes scarce and planning for lunches is necessary.

The walk is best undertaken from spring to early autumn, when the weather is warmer and dryer, days are longer and tourist facilities are fully open. This period is busier, however, and accommodation may be more difficult to find at short notice. In spring the woods are filled with birdsong, leaves on the trees are yet to fully open and the woods are often carpeted with wild flowers. By summer the tree canopy is more established and provides cool shade on hotter days. By autumn the leaves are changing colour and falling, carpeting the floor with rustling leaves whilst colourful fungi are appearing. The season normally starts around Easter then winds down as students return to school in September. Attempts have been made, particularly in coastal resorts, to extend the season by encouraging retired people to come off-season. If walking the route as separate stages, fine days are often seen in winter although daylight hours are much shorter and paths may be much wetter and muddier. Snow is seldom a problem except for the higher ground around Halkyn.

Accommodation

This is unlikely to be a problem in Llandudno, Denbigh, Ruthin and Prestatyn, but elsewhere there may not be a choice of establishments. Possibilities, within a few kilometres, for each stage are given in the text. One way to avoid problems around LlanfairDC, Maeshafn and Brynford is to stay more than one day in the larger towns and use the bus services to move to or from the walk stages;

possibilities are given for each stage. There are very few campsites on the route, other than the larger caravan sites along the coast; examples inland are indicated in the text. All accommodation should be checked in advance.

Transport
There are international airports at Manchester and Liverpool, approximately 1.5 hours away by road.

The main London (Euston) to Holyhead railway line runs along the North Wales coast with mainline stations at Llandudno Junction (spur line to Llandudno), Colwyn Bay, Rhyl and Prestatyn.

Euroroute E22 (Holyhead – Leeds – Amsterdam – and points east) in North Wales is known as the A55 which is essentially a dual carriageway route, also known as the North Wales Expressway. It links to the English motorway network. Of relevance to the North Wales Limestone Way, the road passes through or close to Llandudno Junction (link road to Llandudno), Colwyn Bay, Abergele, St. Asaph and Halkyn.

National Express operates long-distance intercity coach services along the North Wales coast from Prestatyn, Rhyl, Colwyn Bay and Llandudno. A network of local buses connects with train stations and the major towns, although in more rural locations there may be no services. Llandudno, Colwyn Bay, Rhyl, Prestatyn, St. Asaph, Denbigh, Ruthin and Mold are connected by express services, usually one per hour. An indication of useful local services is given for each stage, but all services should be checked first; some services in more rural areas run only on schooldays.

Tourist information centres
Conwy Tourist Information Centre is in Llandudno, Unit 26, Victoria Centre, Mostyn St., Llandudno 01492 577577. There is also a Tourist information point at the Happy Faces Centre in Rhos on Sea 01492 548778 on the Cayley Promenade.

Denbighshire unmanned tourist information points, with tourism leaflets about accommodation, attractions and activities on the route are:

Denbigh Library Hall Square, Denbigh, LL16 3NU, Telephone: 01745 816313

Ruthin Craft Centre, Park Road,

Ruthin, Denbighshire, LL15 1BB is open daily 10am–5.30pm.

Rhyl Tourist Information Centre is a short bus ride from Prestatyn at The Village, West Parade, Rhyl, LL18 1HZ, Telephone: 01745 344515, open Monday to Friday, 9:30am–1pm; 1:30pm–4:30pm.

Flintshire Tourist Information Centre in Mold 01352 759331
www.flintshire.gov.uk/tourism

Refreshments

Food and drink available varies widely day by day. In the main towns of Llandudno, Colwyn Bay, Denbigh, Ruthin and Prestatyn there is normally a wide choice ranging from simple fast food outlets to 4 and 5 star hotels and restaurants. Pubs often provide good, often local, food although many may not be open at lunchtimes. Sadly many rural pubs have recently closed and others reduced their opening hours; some gems remain and are listed in the daily schedules. On some days there will be no refreshments available at lunchtime, other than packed lunches or purchasing food from shops earlier in the day. Vegan or vegetarian meals may be hard to find.

Maps

Maps are not included in this guide. We recommend using the continuously-updated OS online maps via the Ordnance Survey website or app at £4.99/month to £28.99/year, then printing just the areas needed, or downloading to a phone, tablet or GPS device. The seven stages of the route (North Wales Limestone Way Stage 1 of 7 to Stage 7 of 7) are available through the OS maps website; the route for each stage is supplemented by a route card and elevation details; there is even a fly-through facility. GPX files of the route can be exported.

For the more traditional-minded the route is covered by Landranger (1:50K) maps 115, 116 and 117 with 116 covering all but the extreme east and west sections. Explorer (1:25K) maps OL17, 264, 265 and 256 are needed for complete coverage. Ordnance Survey 1:25000 scale maps are most useful as these show field boundaries and more detailed contours. Paper maps will not, of course, show the preferred route.

For the route, start and finish locations, grid references, distances and elevations are taken from the OS online maps. For time calculations the guide uses 4km per hour (2.5 miles per hour) walking speed, adding an additional 10 minutes for each 100m ascent (modified Naismith's Rule). This allows time for looking at the view, chatting with people you meet, bird and flower watching etc. The times will be considered too slow for serious walkers, but too fast for strollers!

In the route descriptions, "paces" refers to "double paces"; treat these as approximate.

Physical features shown on the 1:25000 maps are shown as bold type in the route descriptions.

A basic glossary of the Welsh place names encountered is given in an appendix.

Waymarking

The North Wales Limestone Way is not a national trail, is not waymarked and is not shown on OS maps. For this reason the route descriptions are more detailed than is usual. Local councils are required to signpost all rights of way where they leave a metalled road and the sign must indicate the status of the right of way (e.g. footpath, bridleway or byway). Local authorities are also required to place signs, such as waymarkers, at other locations to assist people who are unfamiliar with the locality. The law requires that stiles and gates be maintained by the landowner in a safe and usable condition. Councils produce a Definitive Map showing rights of way. Conwy (http://www.conwy.gov.uk/en/Resident/Leisure-sport-and-health/Coast-and-Countryside/Public-Rights-of-Way.aspx;) and Flintshire (https://fccmapping.flintshire.gov.uk/connect/analyst/?mapcfg=publicrightsof) have an online version, whereas Denbighshire currently does not (the maps can be examined, by appointment, at council offices in Denbigh). Please notify the relevant council if you come across any path obstructions, impassable stiles or gates, or missing markers.

The North Wales Limestone Way locally intersects national trails and community-based routes; Offa's Dyke Path, North Wales Path, Wales Coast Path, Clwydian Way, North Wales Pilgrims' Way, Hiraethog Trail and some community paths have their own waymarkers.

SSSIs, SACs and nature reserves

The route frequently intersects Sites of Special Scientific Investigation (SSSIs),

Special Areas of Conservation (SACs) and Nature Reserves. The sites are listed for each stage in an Appendix 2, whilst summarised information is given in the route descriptions. For detailed information visit the data sources given below.

Data Sources

Cadw are the Welsh Government's historic environment service and have been used as a basis for the summary information used in the text. Their Cof Cymru (https://cadw.gov.wales/advice-support/cof-cymru/search-cadw-records) is an online service displaying sites across Wales on detailed zoomable OS maps, and providing detailed information.

The Clwyd Powys Archaeological Trust information (http://www.cpat.org.uk) has been used to provide summaries of mines and mining. It lists numerous reports of interest, some of which are available online.

Cyfoeth Naturiol Cymru (Natural Resources Wales) hold information on protected sites such as SSSIs and their website (https://naturalresources.wales/) provides online access to detailed information on those sites. Cyngor Cefn Gwlad Cymru/Countryside Council for Wales was responsible for gathering and collating the information on protected sites; it was incorporated into Cyfoeth Naturiol Cymru (Natural Resources Wales) in April 2013. A synopsis of the information has been used for sites encountered in this walk.

The British Geological Survey (BGS) provide a very useful online viewer of geological maps, linked to information on the geological strata displayed. The 3D Beta version is particularly impressive. Geological faults can be shown and even boreholes. There are links to the BGS Lexicon of named rock units and to borehole charts).

For background information and further reading refer to Appendix 3.

Stage 1: Llandudno, Great Orme to Rhos-on-Sea

Start: Trig point on Great Orme, Llandudno (207m SH 76752 83337)

Finish: Tourist Information Point, Rhos-on-Sea promenade (SH 84238 80506)

Distance: 18.3km (11.4 miles)

Ascent: 581m (1906 feet)

Time: 5 hours 33 minutes

Stage Summary: Start with a descent over grass, paths and down steps to Llandudno then a stroll along the promenade to the next headland ascent. Field and woodland paths with excellent views and a final steep ascent to Bryn Euryn before a gradual descent through streets to the seaside resort of Rhos-on-Sea.

Refreshment: Plenty of choice in Llandudno including Summit Café on Great Orme and Craigside Manor on Little Orme. Pubs in Penrhynside open evenings and weekends only. Bodysgallen Hall Hotel (country house hotel) possible for morning coffee, but lunch tends to be more formal. Rhos-on-Sea has many cafes and a few pubs.

Transport: Llandudno has good links by rail, road and bus. The A55 expressway, a Euroroute (to Holyhead for the Dublin ferry), is linked by a short spur road. The mainline railway (London – Holyhead) also has a short spur (Llandudno Junction to Llandudno). Manchester International Airport is about 1.5 hours away by road. Locally, Arriva Bus Service 12 runs every 15 minutes through to Rhyl, with numerous other services also available.

Accommodation: Plenty of choice in Llandudno, more limited in Rhos-on-Sea. Colwyn Bay offers alternatives.

As a Day Trip: Park the car in Rhos on Sea in the streets away from the promenade, say on Abbey Road. Take a bus 12, 13, 14 or 15 from outside the Cayley Arms on the

promenade to Llandudno alighting at The Palladium on Gloddaeth Avenue, just after travelling down Mostyn St. At the end of the stage there is a short walk back to the car.

Llandudno today is best known as a Victorian seaside resort; it developed from the 1850s when the local landowner, Lord Mostyn, following the Enclosure Act of 1848, settled on the plans for the development of the town as a seaside resort. The Chester – Holyhead railway line opened in 1848; in 1858 a branch line opened into the town and a pier was built. The resort was thus opened up to visitors from northwest England. However the town has a much older history stretching back to the Bronze Age. Extensive copper deposits in the limestones of Great Orme's Head have been mined since 2000BC; excavations since 1987 have discovered over five miles of prehistoric *tunnels. The Romans probably also mined copper here and more modern mining took place from the late 17th to mid-19th centuries. The first historical records indicate that the 6th century St. Tudno brought Christianity to the area from his cell in a hidden cave on the Orme, which still exists. A 12th century church, dedicated to him, though rebuilt in the 15th century, is still in use today.*

Llandudno sits on an isthmus rarely reaching 15 metres (50 ft.) above sea level. To the west, dominating the town, is the massive limestone headland of the Great Orme rising to 207m (679ft.) and to the east is the Little Orme at 141 metres (463ft.). These two limestone headlands, largely cliff-bounded, together define the Llandudno Bay and create a magnificent backdrop to the town.

The Pen y Gogarth/Great Orme is both a Special Area of Conservation (SAC) and a Site of Special Scientific Investigation (SSSI). For the SAC the aim is to control grazing, remove non-native invasive plants and scrub, and manage the feral goat population. The SSSI is important geologically and for its fauna and flora. Historically it has been important for studying the Carboniferous Limestone. The Great Orme Copper Mines are an excellent example of mineralisation of chalcopyrite copper ore in a dolomite matrix.

During the breeding season the cliffs are home to breeding colonies of various kinds of seabirds, including guillemots, razorbills, kittiwakes, cormorants and shags. Choughs may be seen probing the sheep-grazed turf. The thin soils on limestone are home to lime-loving plants such as common and hoary rock rose, thrift, wild thyme, harebell and salad burnet. Globally the only location of the wild cotoneaster, Cotoneaster cambricus, is on the Great Orme cliffs. Many of the lime-loving plants, though not the Cotoneaster, can be seen on the other SSSIs on this walk.

To get to the start of the route from Llandudno town centre there are several options. Walking up should take an hour; several ways are signposted from the town centre. Arriva Bus 26 terminus is close to the Tramway Halfway Station. The **Great Orme Tramway** is the traditional way up, though it operates only in the summer season. A more modern option is the Llandudno Cabin Lift, a mile-long aerial cable car, the longest in the UK, which runs from the Happy Valley close to the town centre right up to the **Summit Complex**. From the Summit Complex, walk the short distance up to the trig point for the start of the stage (207m; 679 feet).

The walk

The first stage of the walk is a descent of the Great Orme into the bustling seaside resort of Llandudno.

From the trig point take one of the grassy paths heading down towards the halfway tram station along the line of the cable car. *As you approach the tram station you may see, off to the right, the old surface mine workings of the 4000 year old **Great Orme Bronze Age Mines**.* Cross a metalled road and pass closely behind the tram station.

Where the main grassy path bears off to the left, head right to cross the stony access track to the farm. Take the wide stony track uphill and curving round to the left. After crossing under the cable cars there is a faint path crossroads; our route goes straight ahead, but the alternatives are worth a look.

*To the left a path leads to the old quarries exposing **Craig Rofft Sandstone**, one of the very few sandstones in the Carboniferous Limestone succession and limited to this small area of the Great Orme.*

The path to the right climbs up to a bluff giving great views down to Llandudno beyond the steep cliff slopes. The curve of the bay with

Halfway Tram Station on Great Orme

Llandudno Bay from Great Orme

The North Wales Limestone Way

the sweep of the Victorian hotels leading round to open fields and the limestone headland of the Little Orme beyond is not to be missed.

Follow the main path down past the tor of **Mynydd Isaf** on your left, to a shallow col (looking out for choughs, with their bright red curved beaks, feeding on the sheep-cropped turf) where a footpath signpost at the junction with the Happy Valley Path points down right towards town. Continue descending steeply right with steps down through the **Happy Valley** Gardens. Look down right to the dry ski slope and toboggan run in the upper part of the valley, then as you descend through a wooden gate into the gardens there are dramatic views down to the pier and sea.

The current Grade II* listed **Llandudno Pier** *or* **landing stage** *was opened to the public on 1st August 1877; an earlier one (1858) was destroyed in a storm. The pier, at 700m long, is the longest in Wales; it is still used by steamers for leisure trips. Cadw regard it as the finest Victorian pleasure pier in Wales.*

The route to the town is well signed, but numerous variations are possible. Perhaps the best is to cross to the road coming down from the ski slope, following this downhill until, with the stone circle on your left (constructed to act as a centre for the Welsh National Eisteddfod ceremonies in 1896 and 1963) take a tarmac path (with handrail) curving right then zig-zagging steeply down to the town, emerging on the road at the Grade II Grand Hotel *(built in 1900, was once the largest hotel in Wales, severely damaged by fire in 1977)*.

Having reached Llandudno, the next phase is a level walk along the hotel-lined promenade, then a climb up the road to the shoulder of the second limestone headland, the Little Orme.

Turn right into Prince Edward Square (war memorial) to join the promenade with the pier entrance on the left. The route goes along the promenade towards the Little Orme, but for shops and restaurants turn right into the town. *Mostyn Street is the main shopping area. The promenade is a pleasant place to eat your lunch, but beware of swooping herring gulls.* Walk along the mid-Victorian hotel-lined promenade for 3km, passing the modern Venue Cymru theatre, as far as the newly opened (2017) lifeboat station *(prior to this opening the lifeboat was stored in the town centre and had to be transported to the North or West Shores by road!*) where you join the pavement opposite Bodafon Fields.

Take the pavement up the Little Orme, passing the house of **Craigside**, then the **Craigside Inn** (originally a farmhouse then briefly a convent) on the right, until it levels out by a footpath sign on the left (North Wales Path and Wales Coastal Path) pointing up the rocky headland of the **Little Orme**.

A short diversion to the summit of the Little Orme is well worth the effort for the views down to Llandudno, although this can be missed out.

Go through the kissing gate on the path, initially uphill, until some fifty paces after a notice board for the North Wales Wildlife Trust's **Rhiwledyn Reserve**, turn sharp left on a well-worn path up a col between the two limestone headlands. Cross the remains of an old, possibly medieval, massive wall then turn left at the top of the col and ascend grassy slopes to the trig point of Little Ormes Head (141m, 463 feet). *There are wonderful views down to Llandudno, across to the Great Orme and beyond.*

Llandudno and Great Orme from Little Orme

The **Creigiau Rhiwledyn/Little Orme's Head SSSI** *occupies the northwestern half of the Little Orme Geologically it is noteworthy for a section through a Carboniferous apron reef structure at the transition from the shelf area southwards to the major basin to the north.*

Plant communities are similar to those of the Great Orme (although not the unique cotoneaster seen there) and breeding guillemots, razorbills, kittiwakes, shags and cormorants are seen here as well. On a recent visit I watched a screaming peregrine being mobbed by a pair of ravens.

The North Wales Limestone Way

Retrace your steps down to the col, with views east over **Penrhyn Bay** and beyond to Rhyl, Prestatyn and the northern foothills of the Clwydian Range. Return to the road, cross to the far pavement, turn left and follow round past the sign "Llandudno Welcomes You".

The next part of the route is on the limestone plateau that overlooks Llandudno, before descending to the outskirts of the village of Llanrhos; much of the route falls within the Creuddyn Peninsula Woods Special Area of Conservation and the Creuddyn SSSI.

The mixed and yew-dominated woodland of the Creuddyn Peninsula are associated with rocky slopes and dry grasslands or scrublands on limestone. The spring is a good time to see wood anemones, wood sanicle, lords-and-ladies, primrose, herb-Robert, enchanter's nightshade, wood avens, woodruff and early purple orchid; bluebells and wild garlic are locally extensive.

Go up Pendre Road towards the old village of **Penrhynside**; 20 metres past the war memorial at a footpath sign on the right take a flight of steps up and then the footpath beyond, curving leftwards to meet a lane. Turn right, then left at a footpath sign on a track behind Mount Pleasant Terrace. In 100m, where the track heads downhill, turn right just before a newly built house, then go half left past an isolated stile, through a kissing gate, and onto open ground using a well-worn path through rough pasture and gorse. From the high point of the path you can detour uphill over limestone pavement and cropped grass to visit the summit (**Mynydd Pant**) – extensive views across to the Little Orme, down to Llandudno Bay and to Anglesey, Puffin Island and Snowdonia).

Return to the path, moving rightwards, then 10m before you are faced by a large gate into a field take the path sharply left through scrub which goes gently downhill to a junction with a well-used path. To the left you can see a kissing gate and a house, but turn sharp right at the junction into a wood. The path runs along the backs of houses, through a kissing gate into the wood proper, with limestone outcrops in the bed of the path. Follow through the wood with fields off to the right passing through a kissing gate into and across a clearing.

When the path descends bear slightly left through trees to a kissing gate with a fine stone wall on the left. At a steel gate go through the kissing gate on the right taking a path right uphill into open pasture with gorse, scattered rowan and silver birch trees. The path meanders through gorse thickets then turns left at a path junction into more open ground. Head diagonally left uphill along a line of electricity poles towards a converted windmill (**Hen Dŵr**, *original mill was probably 17th century, but rebuilt late 18th century*) at the top of the rise. There are great views of the Great Orme, Snowdonia mountains and further east to **Bryn Euryn**. Take the winding well-used path through grassland and gorse of **Nant y Gamar**, bearing left to meet a tarmac lane just before the house/windmill.

Turn right downhill for a few metres then left at a well-built stone wall and along this until forced to move away through grassland and blackberries to reach open ground with views over Llandudno. A marker post ten metres off to the right indicates the path heads downhill half left heading towards the Conwy Valley and mountains. This is a good spot for lunch with fine views to the

Bryniau Tower and Penmaen-bach headland from Nant-y-Gamar

Conwy Valley, the walled town of Conwy and its castle and the Carneddau Mountains.

A few metres further on at another marker post head left, downhill crossing under the crags on a narrow but well-worn path towards a small wooded hill which we'll pass through shortly.

*To the right of this hill, beyond the main road, on a prominent grassy hillock behind a farm is a round tower, **Bryniau Tower**, an early 17th century watchtower similar to those seen later in the walk at Abergele and near*

The North Wales Limestone Way

Whitford. Behind the tower, in the distance, the cliffs of Penmaen-bach, the northernmost extent of the Carneddau Mountains, plunge almost vertically into the sea.

Descend on the path as it curves left round the end of the ridge and when it reaches the junction of two walls go through the kissing gate and along the wall on your right. Shortly after meeting a wall on the left with a grove of yew trees behind, turn right on a stony access track with the buildings of **St David's College** behind a stone wall, now on the left.

The college, a private school, is the former mansion (the 16th century **Gloddaeth Hall**) *of the Mostyn family, important local landowners responsible for the development in the 19th century of Llandudno.*

For a kilometre or so we move off the limestones across the farmlands of the Gloddaeth Syncline, underlain by purple and red sandstones of the younger Carboniferous Gloddaeth Purple Sandstone Formation, to the 17th century Bodysgallen Hall Hotel.

In a few metres go through the kissing gate on the left into an open field and along the well-defined path across the field to the wood beyond (**Coed Gelli** on **Bryn Maelgwyn**). Enter the wood at a stile and go firstly uphill, then down a pleasant woodland path with masses of springtime flowers. When the path leaves the wood go straight ahead down a grassy bank (St. David's College access drive on the left) to join the Llandudno Link Road (A470) at a footpath post.

Cross the road with care to a kissing gate, followed immediately by a wooden stile, into a field/parkland with Llanrhos cemetery to the right. Turn left immediately along the hedge on your left down to the bottom of the field where a stile in the corner gives access to the A470 grass verge. Follow this round to the right, at the roundabout taking the first minor road right. In 50 paces turn right through a wooden five-bar gate (footpath sign) and up the surfaced lane for 50 paces. *On the right is* **Conway Lodge**, *one of the gate lodges to Gloddaeth Hall, dated 1894 with initials HAM, a fine stone-built, red roofed house with black and white upper storey.*

The development of the Llandudno link road somewhat disrupted this access drive. At an old-style signpost (left to Tywyn and Conwy, right to Llandudno) go straight

Conwy Lodge, former gatehouse to Gloddaeth Hall

ahead to a small wooden gate by Oak Cottage which gives access to the B5115.

Cross the road (Pentywyn Road) and turn left on the pavement for about 500 metres crossing back to a narrow pavement at the Robertson company sign (and drive to **Ty'n-y-Coed**).

This geological company started in the Llanddulas limestone quarries east along the coast and relocated here in the early 1970s. It is now a significant local employer with a world class reputation in the oil industry.

At the bottom of the dip, turn left into Bodysgallen Lane to reach the main (fast) road. Cross this carefully, heading up the drive, over a cattle grid towards Bodysgallen Hall Hotel. Avoid the winding hotel drive on your left, but go straight ahead up the steep track towards stone farm buildings. *Note the purple sandstone at the base of the wall on your left. This is the Gloddaeth Purple Sandstone which unconformably overlies the Carboniferous Limestone locally.* At the track junction turn left away from the Spa and up towards the hotel (footpath sign high on the wall of the building ahead). Proceed to the main hotel drive, via a car parking area.

The Grade I listed 17th century **Bodysgallen Hall** *is nowadays a country house hotel. There are exceptional terraced and walled gardens with a parterre. Food is available in the hotel and there is even a boot scraper at the door.*

We now go through the woods and fields of the limestone ridge around Bryn Pydew, following it until its eastern end where it dips to flat fields looking across to the next hill of Bryn Euryn.

The kissing gate directly ahead is a non-public path that avoids the wall stile higher up. Alternatively turn right up the drive

The North Wales Limestone Way

keeping the hotel on your right, bearing left until at a public footpath marker, stones in the wall on your left provide access to the path across the field. This skirts the wood on your right (the **Eastern Covert**) and at the corner of the wood heads straight on across a field to a wooden stile then diagonally left to another kissing gate into a wood. The path ascends gently to a small white cottage on the left (**Goedlodd**).

Head down left on a path, past the front of the cottage garden through a scrubby area and a kissing gate and, ignoring the path which goes left downhill, take the winding, up-and-down, locally muddy, path until this arrives via a ladder stile and gate at a surfaced lane. Turn right up this and at a slight right bend in the road go through a kissing gate and take the path on your left (views left to the offshore wind farm) through grassland with limestone outcrops to reach, in 300m, a kissing gate into a wood. Descend on the path through three more gates until, where a path joins from the left, turn right on the stony track to reach an information board for **Bryn Pydew Nature Reserve** just as cottages appear ahead.

Bryn Pydew is a 4.86 hectare (12 acres) limestone grassland nature reserve managed by the North Wales Wildlife Trust. It is regarded as one of the best sites in Wales to see plants of limestone pavement and grassland, as shown on the information board.

The reserve and quarries are worth a visit, but the route continues between houses to a tarmac road. Turn left, downhill then in a few metres turn right at a footpath sign, through a kissing gate and through a field to another kissing gate. Go alongside the hedge on the right to the narrow field corner, with views across to Penrhynside and the trig point on the Little Orme. Go through the kissing gate, then bear slightly right along the upper edge of the field aiming for the house and tall tree ahead. In the corner of the field there is a waymarker, then a kissing gate onto the stony area between buildings. Take the stony access track with views ahead to Llandrillo yn Rhos parish church *(the church tower was part of the line of signalling stations to warn of 17th century pirates)*, curving to the right with views ahead to **Bryn Euryn**.

Bryn Euryn

A brief walk across the flat fields around the Afon Ganol, underlain by Silurian mudstones, takes us to a steep climb up the hill of Bryn Euryn, capped by the remains of an Iron Age camp. We then descend through open woodland to the streets of Rhos on Sea at the coast.

Go through the kissing gate to join a tarmac lane, heading left downhill for 10 metres to a footpath sign pointing down left through a small steel gate, down a flight of limestone steps, downhill through scrub with occasional steps, through a kissing gate onto a tarmac road. Cross this to an unmarked narrow path, through a kissing gate to a narrow muddy path, over a footbridge across a reedy slow-flowing stream, to a car parking area with sports pitches. Bear half left to a tarmac drive, passing a children's play area on the right. Where the drive meets the residential streets of **Llandrillo yn Rhos** head straight across uphill (on Derwen Avenue) to join Dinerth Road at the top.

Turn right for about sixty paces, turning left up a narrow tarmac lane with footpath sign to Tan y Bryn Road. As the lane bends left, take the footpath on the right through a kissing gate into the woods. In a few metres there is a notice board for Bryn Euryn Local Nature Reserve. The route now ascends the limestone hill of Bryn Euryn. Continue up a flight of steps, bearing left and turning left on a level path.

Bryn Euryn Local Nature Reserve is managed by Conwy Countryside Service as a local nature reserve with woodland and grassland flora (the grassland is an SSSI) typical of limestone terrain.

*The **Bryn Euryn SSSI** is a small site (11.5 hectares, 28 acres) restricted to the slopes and crest of the hill. It is designated for its limestone-based grassland with species similar* *to those of the Great and Little Ormes. Uncommon species include dropwort, white horehound, green-winged orchid with, on the upper slopes, hoary rock rose, yellow-wort, hairy violet, mountain St. John's wort, bloody cranesbill, yew, juniper and the night-flowering Nottingham catchfly which is pollinated by moths.*

At a cross path turn right up the summit trail passing through a grassy area to enter the wood beyond. Bear right here looking for the marker post for the summit trail. The path steepens and comes out of the wood to reveal good views from well-placed seats. As you approach the top of the climb, take time to visit the top of limestone crags below to the right overlooking the narrow valley below along which run the A55 and the mainline railway track.

This has been a strategic route west to Conwy and beyond for 2000 years. In AD61 the Romans marched through here on their way to suppress the Druids in Anglesey, but were ambushed down in the valley and their second-in-command, Sempronius, was killed.

Take the path swinging left which ascends a final steep, partly rocky, section to gain the summit at 131m (365 ft.) with information board and trig point. *The entire summit area is part of an Iron Age hillfort or camp, although you have to look hard to see the remains which are largely obscured by encroaching scrubby vegetation. Views south down the Conwy Valley to the Carneddau Mountains are particularly good.*

To descend, take the grassy path heading north, aiming just right of the Little Orme, to enter the wood at a marker post. The path zig-zags down, joining a cross path where you turn right, heading more gently downhill, for 30 metres, to arrive at a kissing gate and wooden gate by a house on the right.

The ruins of Llys Euryn

Just before the gate there are views through trees down to the golf course and out to sea. An earlier course of the River Conwy can be made out as marshy ground. This was previously navigable; there was a quay from which **Prince Madoc**, *son of Owain Gwynedd, is believed to have sailed with two boats in 1170 across the Atlantic and made land at what is now Mobile Bay, Alabama, thus "discovering" America some 300 years before Columbus. The Welsh migrants are said to have been adopted by the Mandan Indian tribe of Missouri, whose descendants allegedly spoke a form of Welsh. There is little or no direct evidence, although several stone-built forts along rivers into the interior are said to be similar to Owain Gwynedd's birthplace, Dolwyddelan Castle in Snowdonia.*

Turn left just before the gate, down an unmarked path through trees, past houses on the left and an abandoned quarry, dating from the 1840s, down to the right, to suddenly emerge at the ruins of a splendid old stone building, **Llys Euryn**.

Llys Euryn was built on the site of the 13th century mansion of Ednyfed Fychan, chief adviser to Llewelyn the Great. The mansion was burnt down, probably by Owain Glyndŵr, in 1409, but was later rebuilt. The still impressive ruins date to the 15th to 16th century and were inhabited by the Conwys until the time of Charles II.

Take the path round to the right, down several more flights of steps, to arrive at a metalled road with, to the right, a sign for Bryn Euryn Local Nature Reserve. Turn left on the road and in 20 paces at the crossroads go straight across down Rhos Road.

The first prominent stone building on the left, now called Hanover Court, is the converted stable block of a now-demolished 1857 mansion (Bryn Euryn). Many of the buildings you pass are mock Tudor with red tile roofs and black and white "timbered" upper storeys, but several smaller fishermen's and quarrymen's cottages, dating to the 1850s, remain.

Follow Rhos Road, past houses, shops and cafes, to the end of the stage at the tourist information point on the promenade, slightly to the right of its junction with Rhos Road. *The point is open 10am till 4pm, though closes early if slack.*

Rhos-on-Sea is a bustling seaside village, particularly during holiday periods when the promenade and streets are busy with visitors. If you have time, you may wish to visit **St.**

St. Trillo's Chapel, Rhos-on-Sea

Trillo's Chapel, *500m to the north along the promenade. It is believed to be the smallest church in the British Isles, seating only six people. The original cell of the Celtic St Trillo was 6th century, but the building has been much rebuilt and repaired over the years.*

On the way back to Rhos-on-Sea centre, take the footpath along the sea wall. At low tide you can see the remains of the **Royal Fishing Weir**, *also known as Rhos Fynach fishing weir, a structure which predated the Magna Carta (1215AD). The weir was extremely effective until the early 20th century; one night in 1850 there was a record catch of 35000 herring, and in 1907 ten tons of mackerel were caught in a single night. The weir fell into disuse in the First World War and the wooden stakes were later removed as a hazard to boats.*

As you head back towards the Information Point, you pass on the right the **Rhos Fynach Tavern** *(pub and restaurant) which is one of the oldest buildings in Rhos-on-Sea, with features dating back to the 15th century. The land on which it stands was granted to a Captain Henry Morgan (a buccaneer, not the notorious pirate Captain Morgan) by the Earl of Leicester in 1575.*

The Rhos-on-Sea **Breakwater** *was completed in 1984 in an attempt to stop the repeated sea flooding when the sea wall was breached in winter storms. It is a useful mooring place for small boats.*

Stage 2: Rhos-on-Sea to Abergele

Start:	Tourist Information Point, Rhos-on-Sea promenade (SH 84238 80506)
Finish:	Abergele "Tesco Roundabout" (SH 94341 77616)
Distance:	17.3km (10.8 miles)
Ascent:	540m (1771 feet)
Time:	5 hours 13 minutes

Stage Summary: Starts with a gentle stroll along the coastal promenade then up a wooded stream, across a golf course and steeply up to the limestone ridge of Mynydd Marian at 207m (682 ft.). Fine scenic open grassland paths and steep ascents and descents through fields and woods finishing with a descent through woodland paths and surfaced footpaths along the back ways of Abergele.

Refreshment: Plenty of cafes and a few pubs in Rhos-on-Sea and in Colwyn Bay; refreshment kiosks and Porth Eirias along the promenade. MASH Micropub on the outskirts of Llysfaen is open Wednesday to Sunday from noon. There is a shop with long opening hours just off-route in Llysfaen. Numerous shops, cafes and pubs in Abergele.

Transport: The Arriva No. 12 service runs from Llandudno to Rhyl, passing through Rhos-on-Sea and Abergele. It runs every 15 minutes in each direction and has on-board wifi.

Accommodation: Hotels, guesthouses and B&B in Rhos-on-Sea, Colwyn Bay and Abergele.

As a Day Trip: Park the car in side streets away from the promenade and walk to the tourist information point on the promenade. At the end of the stage take a bus back to the start (No. 12 is the most frequent).

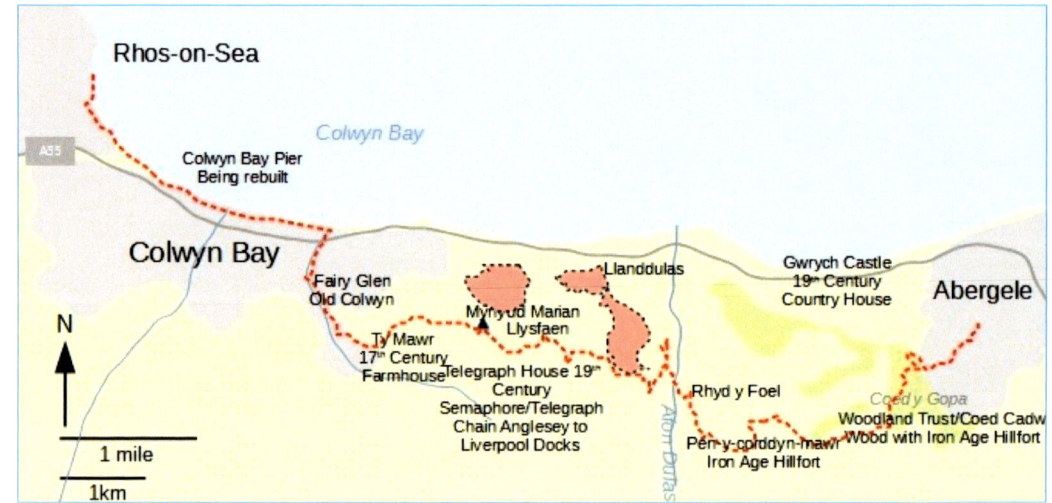

The walk

The first phase of the walk follows the promenade around the gentle curve of Rhos Bay as far as Old Colwyn.

Take the promenade east along the **North Wales Path** and Wales Coast Path with, to the right, *Aberhod Old Hall, a 17th century farmhouse, now converted into housing, though with the frontage preserved. Left of this is the* **Harlequin Puppet Theatre**, *the first and only purpose-built puppet theatre in the UK. There are several prom shelters and a couple of kiosks serving refreshments. Houses on the landward side are now well set back behind the big grassy bank of the Cayley Promenade. The prom has been recently redeveloped with new paving, seating and small wavy walls of rough granite blocks alternating with black polished limestone with shells and coral pieces. The limestone is from the Carlow/Kilkenny region of southeast Ireland, but is similar to the limestones of this walk. There are also 12 granite "postcards" on the promenade, each depicting an interesting aspect of local history. Each has an adjacent QR code.*

Life-size silhouette statues on Colwyn Bay promenade

The quarried cliffs of Penmaenhead and the Rainbow Bridge

The former **Victoria Pier** partly collapsed in a winter storm of 2017 and was finally demolished in 2018. A "short pier" in the style of the original is being constructed. Opposite the pier is a subway through to the largely Victorian **Colwyn Bay** with amenities including the train station, buses, shops and restaurants.

Continue past Porth Eirias with its upmarket refreshment options. The prom narrows after this and the sea encroaches, but a higher path behind the wall on the right of the road is a safe option if waves are breaking over the prom.

Where the road bends right under a six-arch stone railway viaduct, turn inland on the **North Wales Path**. The **Wales Coast Path** and cycleway continue eastwards along the promenade, passing the Rainbow Bridge across the North Wales Expressway.

Historically the limestone cliff came down to the sea at Penmaenhead forming a partial barrier to east-west movement along the coast., but now after much quarrying, road and railway building it is barely noticeable, with just a little pinnacle of rock remaining dipping its toe in the sea.

On this headland in 1399 King Richard II,

returning to England from Ireland, was ambushed on the tricky headland path by supporters of Henry Bolingbroke. Richard was taken to Flint Castle, then in stages to London where he was kept in the Tower and "persuaded" to hand over the crown to Bolingbroke who was crowned Henry IV (establishing the House of Lancaster) a fortnight later. This ended the direct line of Plantagenet kings who had ruled England for 250 years. A few months later Richard died as a prisoner in the Lancastrian stronghold of Pontefract Castle, probably due to starvation. Henry's claim to the throne was questionable and years later the Yorkists initiated the bloody Wars of the Roses in order to secure the crown. This event probably also set the scene for Owain Glyndŵr's rebellion of September 1400; Glyndŵr had been a supporter of Richard II, whereas under Henry IV he fell into disfavour. A local land dispute with Baron Grey de Ruthyn (an associate of Henry's) escalated and led to warfare including the sacking of Ruthin.

This next stage follows a small river up through Old Colwyn, then along a delightful wooded glen before climbing high onto the limestone ridge of Mynydd Marian overlooking the sea and the peaks of Snowdonia.

Go under the viaduct and up Beach Road along the riverside. As you near Old Colwyn, take a path through the tunnel under the main road. Follow the waymarked path up the Fairy Glen by the side of the river, until joining Coed Coch Road. Cross this and, going right, shortly take a footpath on the left, bending right around the edge of a golf course. Cross Peulwys Lane and another section of golf course to reach a stone track by tall trees. Turn left, uphill, but where the North Wales Path turns right, continue uphill through a farm gate, increasingly steeply, to a more open gorse-studded hillside and into the parish of Llysfaen.

***Llysfaen** is a collection of farms and houses built around "The Marian" with its poorly-defined centre at the church on the north side. In addition to the farms it was important for small-scale quarrying of limestone, particularly on the southern slopes of the Marian, for building stone and lime burning. On old maps numerous lime kilns are indicated, but few survive today. The village has grown with the continuing development of housing estates over the past 100 years.*

Outcrop of Silurian mudstones beside the path

Loose block of rippled sandstone from Ffernant Formation

At the top of the steep slope the track bends sharp left below an outcrop of Silurian mudstones. *There are fine views here back down to Colwyn Bay, Rhos on Sea and beyond.* The path now heads to the edge of the field, bending right uphill alongside the hedge. At the top of the second field pass through the kissing gate at a path junction. Head straight across the farm track, taking a hidden path rightwards behind a hedge, along a tunnel of trees, rather than the open field beyond the farm gate on the right.

Bedded limestone forms the bank on the left, but the reddish-purple colour of the soils below indicates this is the base of the Carboniferous Limestone where it overlies the **Ffernant Formation** *sandstones and mudstones (the old Basement Beds) which form the fields sloping down to the right.*

Emerging from the tunnel, go straight across at the metal-bar stile, keeping the old drystone wall on the left, with open sea views beyond the housing estate, to a ladder stile to pass behind and round two warehouse-type buildings. Emerge into a small industrial estate with the Conwy Brewery and its micropub on the right.

Spring cowslips on Mynydd Marian

Go through the concrete yard (the old house ahead on the right is **Ty Mawr**, a Grade II listed 17th century farmhouse) bearing left down a concrete drive between ruined buildings, then turning sharp right up through a small wood. Take the concrete drive left to reach the road, turn right and in 50m sharply left steeply up a short tarmac drive, and left along a stony track. In 50m turn right uphill between large quarried blocks onto the Colwyn County Borough Council's **Mynydd Marian** Nature Reserve.

Climber on Castle Inn Quarry

This 14.2 hectare (35 acre) SSSI comprises limestone grassland (with flowers including hoary rock rose, spring cinquefoil as well as orchids of various species, cowslips, harebells, and wild thyme). It also has populations of the dwarf race of the silver studded blue butterfly which had been introduced into the Dulas Valley to the east and subsequently migrated here.

The next stage stays high on the open ridge before dropping down through woods to a steep-sided river valley, the Afon Dulas. A brief spell on roads and wooded paths along the flat valley floor takes us to a climb to spectacular cliffs and screes, circling round the defences of an Iron Age hillfort.

The route goes along the crest of the hill with extensive views in all directions. *The hills of Snowdonia, the Great Orme, the Clwydian Range, Isle of Man, Lake District and – on a clear day – Blackpool Tower are all visible, as well as the offshore wind farms and oil/gas platforms.* As the slope eases, head to the right of a trig point (208m, 682 ft. (inaccessible behind steel railings) and pass along the top of the Castle Inn Quarry, a well-used climbing venue.

A useful panoramic painting is by the fence at the top of the crags. Several seats allow restful appreciation of the views. On the top of the hill are two covered reservoirs which supply the village. Beyond these is the Grade II listed **Telegraph House**, *part of the chain of semaphore signalling stations built in 1841, later converted to telegraph use, which relayed messages from Anglesey to Liverpool Docks.*

Pass to the right of Telegraph House and bear left to join a stony track. Take one of the grass paths half left down to the car park then exit to Bron y Llan Rd. Turn left and go downhill to the crossroads.

Diagonally opposite is **St. Cynfran's Church**, *believed to have developed from a 777 AD site, with the current building in part dating to the 13th century.* **St. Cynfran's Well**, *100m north of the church, but on private ground, was still supplying holy water to the church font into the 20th century.*

Turn right on the main road, downhill, past the school and then Gadlas Rd., turning left in 40m down a track through a rock cutting. In a few metres fork left along the footpath and with a wall on the right

Carneddau Mountains from Maiden's Leap

The North Wales Limestone Way

and the backs of houses on the left continue on the stony path (originally the access drive to *Plas yn Llysfaen, a mainly 19th century grand house with 17th century northwest wing*) past limestone outcrops on the right to meet a stony vehicle track with a playground straight ahead.

Turn right up the track (shops are visible just past the playground), flanked on the left by a line of fine old beech trees, then at the farm building on the right fork left along a wooded path which skirts **Plas Farm**. Swing left before the gate, then bend right at the security fence for the quarry, through a gate, emerging into open grassland with a fenced quarry/landfill site on the left. Keep the fence on your left through another gate and as the fence veers off to the left make for the unmarked highest point ahead (**Craig y Forwyn**, *Maiden's Leap, named after a young lass falling or jumping from the cliff to her death.*). Beware the unprotected cliff edge in front of you.

There are views down into the Dulas Valley, out to sea and of the Clwydian Hills and Snowdonia mountains.

The walk now moves through parts of the **Llanddulas Limestone and Gwrych Castle Wood SSSI.** *Broad-leaved woodland is present below the screes, with thinner limestone soils on the plateaux supporting limestone grassland. The local deeper soils, often on glacial till, support bracken, gorse and locally heather. Craig y Forwyn woods are an ancient woodland site with silver birch, oak, ash, beech and sycamore. On the cliff faces there are yew, spindle, and the nationally scarce rock whitebeam. The shrub layer comprises hazel, hawthorn, wild privet, spurge laurel, spindle, yew and ash regeneration. Infestation by ivy is common and the invasive cotoneaster is common on scree slopes. The mosaic of habitats supports various butterflies including the scarce silver studded blue, pearl-bordered fritillary, silver-washed fritillary, white-letter hairstreak, green hairstreak, brown argus and moths such as the scarce plume moth, cistus forester and chalk carpet.*

Across the steep-sided Dulas Valley to the southeast there is another limestone plateau; a thin line of what looks like a bank of scree running across the plateau from the cliff edge in the southwest to the northeast is actually the northwestern rampart of the Iron Age **Pen y Corddyn Mawr Hillfort**; *our way shortly traverses the base of the screes below the cliffs on the south side. This impressive 10 hectare (25 acre) hillfort (similar in size to the better-known Moel Fenlli in the Clwydian Hills near*

Pen y Corddyn Mawr Hillfort and cliffs from across the Dulas Valley

Ruthin) is defended by cliffs on three sides and by double banks and ditches on the fourth. It is deemed to be Iron Age, although finds of Roman coins and other artefacts suggest re-use during Roman times. Note that the fort is on private land.

From the top retrace your steps for ten metres then turn (south) steeply downhill, between the steep rocks on the left and a bank of gorse on the right, aiming towards a finger post on the North Wales Path.

Bear left downhill on this path along the base of a scree slope with the impressive crags of the upper tier of Craig y Forwyn towering above and a view down the Dulas Valley to the sea. Pass through a wooden gate in an old wall with woods below to the right, then, levelling out, on an old tramway route, into a delightful wood, leaving the old tramway by turning right steeply downhill immediately after the second rock cutting, on a well-worn path to a narrow road and lay-by.

Turn right along Cwymp Road past "Dulas Bach" along the base of the wood (looking out for alpacas in the fields down to the left), forking left at 300m/5 minutes and descend through fern-rich woods to cross the **Afon Dulas** and steeply up past Cwymp Mill. Take the footpath signposted right along the access road to "Country View" then at the gates fork right on a path through the wood, crossing one stile and climbing gently to a gate onto the road at the **Rhyd y Foel** village sign. Turn left, and in 30 paces cross the road to a stile at the base of a slope. Head steeply uphill, winding through sparse woodland, before veering left then turning right at a fence boundary to meet the cotoneaster-covered screes from the cliffs above.

Follow the cropped grass path as it rises gently with patches of heather, cotoneaster

North Wales Path signpost below the upper tier of Craig y Forwyn

Rock cutting on the old tramway route above the Dulas Valley

and gorse, beneath the limestone crags and scree (the defences of Pen-y-Corddyn Mawr hillfort) until the path meets a fence descending from the left and bears slightly right to enter an old walled or banked enclosure. A defined path – possibly a sheep track – goes down the middle of the enclosure, exiting through a break in the bank at the far end, where on the left are the bramble-covered remains of old buildings (shown as Pen-y-Corddyn on the first edition OS map). Descend a grassy path along the base of the crags, through a stile by a gate, then level out, curving left, through a wood, with fence and field on your right. An old well to the right of the path has a spring draining into a muddy pond.

After descending from the limestone ridge of Pen y Corddyn Mawr we cross often wet fields to reach another wooded limestone hill, again topped by an Iron Age hillfort. This is descended on good paths to Abergele where surfaced paths take us on back ways to the end of the stage.

Pass a whitewashed cottage on your

Cliffs and screes forming the southern rampart of Pen y Corddyn Mawr Hillfort

right to reach a stile by an old outbuilding of **Garth Gogof**. *Here the path leaves the Clwyd Limestones for the underlying Carboniferous Ffernant Formation mudstones until Coed y Gopa. These rocks are rarely exposed, but the deep red colour of the soil in the fields is characteristic. The OS map shows a number of wells or springs and the going can be extremely wet. As you traverse the fields ahead after rain, it is even possible to hear water seeping up through the soil.*

Go down the grassy slope to the lane, turn right into the farmyard (cars parked on left) to the waymarker on a wooden gatepost pointing diagonally right through a steel gate (no stile) into a paddock. Beyond the paddock go over the stile on the left, then alongside the edge of the field until, where the hedge bends sharply left, take a faint path straight across the open field – masked by the barley in the summer – to a stile in the hedge.

In the next field aim diagonally right downhill for a footpath pole near a gap in the hedge ahead. Cross the stile into the lane and immediately the stone stile into the next field, still southeast, but with the slightly wavy hedge on your right. Go through the gate at the corner of the field

Spring wood anemones on the path descent to the Dulas Valley

then as you approach **Betws Lodge Wood**, head uphill to meet the corner of the wood and a bridleway.

Go along the edge of the wood (a wonderfully wild wood with contorted trees, yews, ivy everywhere and limestone outcrops), then through a gate into the farmyard bearing slightly right down a concrete ramp between farm buildings. Turn sharp left at the bottom, past the front of the farmhouse (**Tyddyn-uchaf**) and old barn, then sharp right along a stony track to join a lane.

As the lane turns sharp right, take the stile ahead into Coed Gopa/Gopa Wood, managed by Coed Cadw/the Woodland Trust, and head steeply uphill to join a forestry track.

The 36.3 hectare (90 acre) **Coed y Gopa SSSI** *is noted for its fauna and flora, including a winter roost of the lesser horseshoe bat. Although a plantation of beech and Scots pine clothes the hill, other trees and plants indicate that at least the northern part of the plantation is an ancient woodland site. Ash, silver birch, spindle, buckthorn, wild privet and yew are in addition to woodland herbs such as stinking hellebore and spurge laurel. Grassland areas contain plants typical of thin limestone soils; common rock rose, salad burnet, wild thyme, fairy flax and early purple orchid.*

Turn left downhill, but in 80 paces take the path forking right through the trees, mostly downhill. *To visit the two hectare (5 acre) Iron Age hilltop fort of* **Castell Cawr**, *a scheduled ancient monument, take an unmarked, though obvious, track uphill to the right, and through a gap in the trees, crossing the outer banks of the fort to an information board and the hillfort itself where the trees have been cleared from the top.*

Return the same way, turning right on

Searching for the path through the barley field

the main path then sharp left at a waymarked path junction, dropping down to cross a footbridge over a narrow ravine, then bearing right down a track which steepens, becomes rocky and slippery.

The ravine, **Ffos y Meiddiaid**, *is 3-5m wide, 7m deep and runs for some 300m. It is a lead and copper mining cut of medieval, possibly Roman, age worked out by the 19th century, and now provides roosting sites for bats, including the lesser horseshoe bat.*

The path eventually joins a forest track where you turn right downhill, round a hairpin bend (*where there is a seat with good views over Abergele to Rhyl, the sea, the coastal plain and the end of the Clwydian Hills at Prestatyn*). As the track bends left at **Copa'r Wylfa**, take a flight of wooden steps down right through the trees to a lane where it joins the Tan y Gopa Road at a Coed y Gopa information board.

Turn right along the lane and as it steepens and bears right take the surfaced footpath signed to the left between houses. Where the path meets a road, turn left along the road, turning right at the next road junction, then in 20m turn left down another tarmac path. Take this series of paths, some tarmac, some stony, through the housing development of **Tan-y-Gopa** until the path comes out at a roundabout on the A547 main road opposite Tesco and a bus shelter, convenient for the end of this stage.

Abergele is a small town, for centuries a market town until the livestock market moved out in 1996 – and the site is now a supermarket. It contains many old buildings, hotels, churches, pubs and halls with more modern housing developments. It has rounded hills behind the steep-sided limestone plateaux inland and the low-lying coastal plain dipping down to the sea and beaches at Pensarn. It has a history of farming, mining and quarrying. There are shops, restaurants and a few hotels and guesthouses. There are good bus connections along the coast to east and west with the mainline train station at Pensarn, just to the north. The A55 expressway bypasses the town.

Stage 3: Abergele to Denbigh

Start:	Abergele "Tesco Roundabout" (SH 94341 77616)
Finish:	Denbigh Castle (SJ 01573 65859)
Distance:	21.6km (13.4 miles)
Ascent:	642m (2105 feet)
Time:	6 hours 27 minutes

Stage Summary: Starts with footpaths through the village then field paths with a steep, locally stepped, climb through a wood to a watchtower and field paths. There follows a long section on minor roads, interspersed with field and wood paths, into the picturesque Elwy Valley. Minor roads down and out of the wooded valley lead to the old village of Henllan, then field paths, tracks and woods to the outskirts of Denbigh. Well-surfaced paths with views of Denbigh Castle lead to an ascent on back streets to the castle. Some of the paths are not well used and may be difficult to penetrate.

Refreshment: There are several pubs, shops and cafes in Abergele, but then nothing until Henllan where there is a community shop. The Llindir Inn in Henllan is open 5pm – 11pm Monday to Wednesday, and 12 noon till late the rest of the week. Meals are available except Mondays. Denbigh has numerous shops, pubs and eating places.

Transport: Abergele has good links by rail, road and bus. Arriva Service 12 runs every 15 minutes through to Llandudno and Rhyl. Arriva Service 13 connects at Bodelwyddan to Service 51 to Denbigh. There is an infrequent bus service Henllan – Denbigh.

Accommodation: The tourist information office in Denbigh Library is a good place to check. The Guildhall Tavern (formerly the Bull Inn) is the most historic hotel in Denbigh still offering accommodation; the Crown Hotel was a historic "Whig Inn" but is currently closed. The Grade II listed Bull

The North Wales Limestone Way

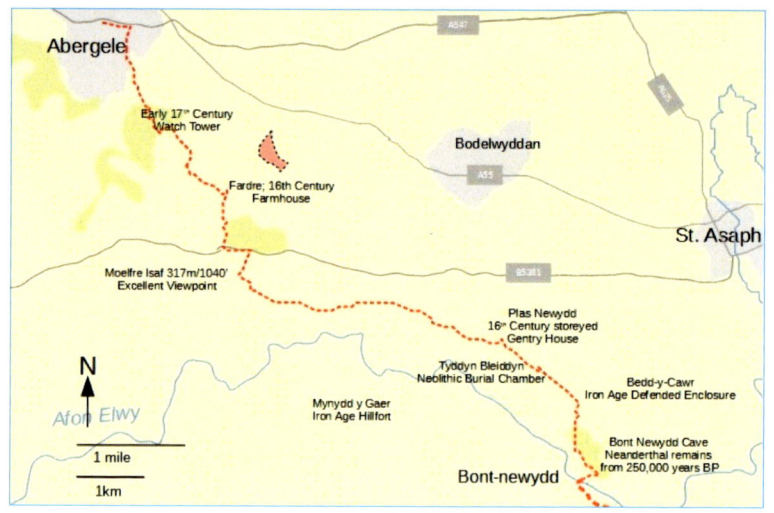

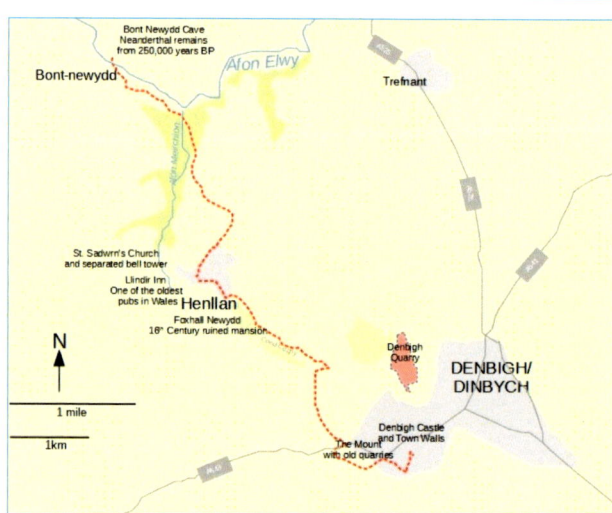

was a probably 17th century (or earlier) timber-framed building that has been altered over the years. There are several B&B's in town.

As a Day Trip: Park the car in a side street or in Water Street car park (pay) and walk to the start of the stage. At the end of the stage take the 51 Rhyl bus from Hall Square (making sure you get the correct side of the street). Change at Ysbyty Glan Clwyd for the No. 13 to Llandudno, alighting in Abergele.

The walk

Stage 3 initially follows a stream up through the outskirts of Abergele, across fields to the start of a steep climb up through woods onto a limestone ridge, on top of which sits a 17th century watchtower. Farmland and minor roads lead to the crest of a ridge descending from Moelfre Isaf and overlooking to the south the quiet picturesque wooded Elwy Valley.

From **Abergele** "Tesco Roundabout" head east on the A547 through the town centre, turning right on Glanrafon just before a small bridge over the Afon Gele across which is the distinctive 1880 Grade II listed St. Paul's Wesleyan Methodist Chapel. Where this road turns right, take a signed footpath straight ahead (heading south), at first between houses, then alongside the stream crossing a footbridge, until the path forks left through a kissing gate, diagonally uphill across an open field on a slightly worn path to a kissing gate in the left corner to join a narrow lane. There are good views back over Abergele and the sea beyond.

Turn left and in 25 paces take the signed footpath right into the woods of **Coed Abergele** where paths and steps lead steeply up through drifts of wild garlic, wood anemones, dog's mercury and scarce orchids. Keep heading uphill in a southerly direction, turning left where the steps end at a prominent cross-path, then right in a few paces into a conifer-dominated wood. The gradient eases towards the summit of **Tower Hill** (179m, 587 ft.) then the woods end at farmland; here the path turns left through the trees until a kissing gate on the right gives access to the tower in the field a few tens of metres ahead.

The **Tower** *is an early 17th century circular tower considered to be a watchtower*

The old watchtower on the hill above Abergele

The North Wales Limestone Way

to warn of raiding by Barbary pirates or corsairs from the sea. It is similar to the better known one near Whitford (seen on Stage 7 of this walk) and the one at Bryniau, Llanrhos (seen from Stage 1).

Return to the wood taking the path right (east) through the wood edge to the corner then across a stile back into the field. Head downhill with gorse and hedge on your left to join a tractor track passing a mobile phone mast then through a kissing gate to join a stony farm track which leads in 50 metres up to a minor road.

Turn right and in 25 paces cross the stile to take the almost hidden path (footpath sign) on the left just past the access drive to Warren Cottage, but immediately before the substantial wrought iron gates of the next house. Go southeast along the enclosed path until it reaches a stile into an open field (currently the two markers – one pointing straight ahead and one pointing right – are missing). Turn right slightly downhill skirting the scrub on your right with views ahead to the upstanding **Moelfre Isaf** (317m, 1040 ft.). At the next field corner there is a stile with waymarker and beyond this keep the hedge on your right. Head south, climbing over or under any electric fences, until the next field corner where a hidden stile is marked by a large stone at its foot. Head half left (southeast) across the field aiming for the left-most of a line of three or four trees in the far hedgerow. Cross the stile inset from the field corner and continue along the field edge with the hedge on your right, ignoring any openings to the field and track on the right.

Several electric fences may be in your way; avoid these by stepping over, rolling under or using the insulated spring clip.

Looking back to the watchtower from the south

44   *The North Wales Limestone Way*

Over the fields to the left is an old farmhouse with strikingly tall chimney stacks. This is **Fardre** *(or Fadre) farmhouse, a Grade II* listed 16th century stone-built dwelling, the seat of an important Denbighshire gentry family.*

There are views beyond to the Clwydian Hills and behind to the grassy hill of **The Warren**. Go under electricity lines to reach a tractor track at the bottom of the field. Turn left for 30 paces to a footpath pole hidden in the hedge and, 5 paces beyond, pass through a set of twin gates to the minor road.

The 16th century farmhouse of Fardre

The low point in the road marks the change from the Clwyd Limestone underfoot to the older Basement Beds of the Carboniferous (now known as the Ffernant Formation), then, nearing the junction with the main road, to Silurian mudstones.

Turn right along the road, initially slightly downhill then, crossing a stream, uphill past forestry (**Coed Pen-y-Bryn**) on the left until it joins the B5381 in about 10 minutes. *Note that the telephone box shown here on OS maps no longer exists.*

Turn left on the B5381; although it's a B road the traffic can be fast-moving. The southern (far) verge is safer and faces the oncoming traffic.

This road is widely referred to as a Roman Road, even on OS maps, and is believed to be the route from Deva (Chester) to Segontium (Caernarfon), although no evidence of Roman structure has yet been documented.

Take the first minor road on the right along the eastern edge of a wood and under the first set of power lines. Just after Ty'n y Mynydd turn left down the drive to the house **Talgrwn Bach** as far as the yard. Turn left here (waymarker) then sharp right just beyond the dog pound. Go along the top of the field with great views (do not go downhill) heading east southeast then cross the two stiles on the right into the next field with pylon straight ahead. Turn left, alongside the hedge on the left, through an opening in the hedge ahead to the next field then on to massive stones in the field corner against a wood (which is shown on the Landranger maps but not the Explorers). Cross a somewhat precarious stile into the wood, then keep the hedge to your left as the path meanders through the trees reaching a large sycamore on the left where a newly-constructed stile on the left is crossed into a field. Turn right keeping along the edge of the field, with masses of gorse to the left, to the corner where you cross the stile (footpath post) to join a minor road.

Ignore roads to left and right and go straight across down the eastern ridge of **Moelfre Isaf** with the quiet wooded Elwy Valley to the right, *beyond which is the bracken-clad, steep-sided isolated hill of **Mynydd y Gaer** with its (probable Iron Age) hillfort*. Ignore roads to left and right, staying parallel to the power lines on your right, with good views north to the sea, south inland and east to the Clwydian Hills. The road continues for about 2km, across a small valley/stream (*The **Nant-Luke**, a tributary of the Elwy; this is the county boundary, so you move from Conwy into Denbighshire*) by **Nant Bach** again with good views where hedges permit.

Just after this stream, where a minor road comes in from the left, you move back from the older Silurian mudstones to the Carboniferous Clwyd Limestone Group, which continues to Henllan and Denbigh.

The route continues along the side of the Elwy Valley through fields and woods, much of it on minor roads, until it descends past the internationally famous Bont Newydd Cave to cross the river at Bont Newydd. A climb on wooded lanes takes us to the limestone village of Henllan with its old houses, church and thatched pub.

At the farm road for **Bryn Hen** turn right down the track, but about 25m before the farm buildings go left through a gate into a field. The path is faint, but head east, aiming for the large tree in the far field boundary (about halfway down the field). Watch out for electric fences. Cross the stile or go through a gate into the next field passing a capped shaft (*an air shaft for the* *old Cefn/Plas Newydd – lead/silver mine worked from early 18th century until 1865)*, heading to the stile halfway down the field boundary – taking care when crossing electric fences. Enter the next field through a gap in the fence with woods down to the right and aim for the tall chimneys of the grand house (**Plas Newydd**) ahead. Head for a marked stile halfway down the field just to the left of a line of three trees, then across this alongside the hedge on your left to cross another stile in the top left corner. Turn left up the hedge to just before a new farm track with wood behind, where you turn right in the field with electric fence and farm track on your left.

Behind the wood is Plas Newydd, a Grade II* listed Elizabethan gentry house built in 1583. The house is largely unaltered and represents a fine example of the house type adopted by the North Wales gentry of the period.

As the track bends left, bear right, aiming for a stile in the wall ahead with a modern farm building beyond. Turn left over the stile and head uphill on a path/track to join the minor road, passing the impressive stone Great Danes guarding the driveway to **Plas Hafod** kennels. Turn right and in 0.5km the road bends sharp left uphill past **Ysgubor Newydd** then bends right under the wooded hill of **Cefn Meiriadoc**.

Just past the house at the junction there are the remains of **Tyddyn Bleiddyn** *a Neolithic or Bronze Age chambered cairn (an oval grassy mound 26m by 12m with just a few large stones visible) below in the field. This was excavated in 1869 and 1871 when two chambers, approached by passages, were found with many crouched inhumations.*

In just under 1km turn right on another minor road then the road bends left and in 50m take the footpath through a wooden gate on the right. The well-used path enters the deciduous wood of **Coed yr Accar**, part of the **Coedydd Ac Ogofau Elwy A Meirchion/Lower Elwy and Meirchion Woods and Caves SSSI** and heads downhill to emerge on a narrow lane just before a derelict house with a pond.

The SSSI comprises semi-natural broadleaved woodland with a rare flowering plant assemblage, scarce bryophyte assemblage (mosses, liverworts and hornworts) and features of geological and palaeontological interest. In addition to the nationally important Bont Newydd Cave, others contain

The blocked up entrance to the Bont Newydd Cave, formerly home to Neanderthals

The Afon Elwy in Bont Newydd

Ice Age animal bones, but no human remains. Trees and plants are those typical of these limestone habitats, although the wild service tree and small-leaved lime are unusual.

Just past the pond fork left on the road for 100 paces to a footpath down to the right which you return to shortly. The nationally important **Bont Newydd Cave** is some 40 paces past the footpath in the cliff above the road, south-facing under a rock overhang.

It is a Scheduled Monument on Cefn Estate ground and the entrance is bricked up with a steel door, but it is interesting to observe its position overlooking the River Elwy which would have been ideal for watching game movements. Archaeological excavations here produced the earliest hominid remains (notably an early Neanderthal tooth 250,000 years old) found in Wales, together with flints including hand axes, scrapers and Levallois flakes (flakes produced by flint knapping that could later be turned into various tools). The earliest modern humans came to Europe about 40,000 years ago, so the Neanderthals would have been here for 200,000 years before then!

Retrace your steps west and take the footpath left through the wood down to join the minor road by the old post office and so to the 18th Century bridge in **Bont Newydd** where the clear waters of the **Afon Elwy**, which form the county boundary, flow over flat-lying limestone slabs.

Turn left over the bridge, ignoring the steep uphill lane off right. For about a kilometre the road runs above the delightful Afon Elwy, with woods on the right (**Coed y Dafarn**), and impressive limestone crags (**Cefn Crags**) on the hillside north, passing an outdoor centre, until at **Pont y Trap** the lane crosses the **Afon Meirchion** and swings uphill through the woods of **Coed y Trap**.

The steep wooded cleft of the Afon Meirchion, along the line of the Cefn Fault, lies down to the right, but contains no continuous public rights of way. Warning signs about high-powered rifles in use (for controlling fallow deer) will, in any case, be enough to deter walkers.

Climb steeply uphill through woods, away from the Afon Meirchion, and turn right at the B5428. Where a minor road comes in from the left there is a driveway on the right through parkland to the substantial house of **Garn** (dated 1739). Continue on the B5428 into the medieval

The south-facing Cefn Crags in the Elwy Valley

Grade II listed cottages in School Street, Henllan

The free-standing square bell tower of St. Sadwrn's Church, Henllan

The reputedly haunted Llindir Inn, Henllan

village of **Henllan**, with its grey limestone buildings, bearing left down School Street to reach a meeting of five roads.

School Street contains five Grade II listed houses; the first two were originally a single dwelling dating from the mid-18th century (one house dated 1752 over a window – its original doorway) set back from the lane. The other three are a mid 19th century (one dated 1864) terrace, opening directly onto the street.

An interesting diversion here is to turn right on Church Street, view the church, return forking right down the alley to visit Llindir Inn, then uphill on Llindir Street to join Denbigh Road.

Turning right on Church Street leads to St. Sadwrn's Church. A Celtic Llan was established on the site in the 6th or 7th century by St. Sadwrn. The current Grade II* listed building is largely of early 19th century construction (1806) and replaces a medieval one (13th or 14th century, although little remains from this period). Within the churchyard there are further Grade II listed items; three 17th century chest tombs and a *group of four vault structures dating from the early 19th to very early 20th century, centred on a fine pyramidal vault to the Heaton family of Plas Heaton, one kilometre to the northeast. The Grade II* listed four-stage square bell tower is separate from the church on a raised rock, apparently to increase the range of the bells across the village – and possibly act as a defensive peel tower as required. The churchyard walls, probably 18th and 19th century with lych-gate (1935) are also Grade II listed.*

The Grade II listed **Llindir Inn** *is said to be one of the oldest pubs in Wales. The original building, possibly a farmhouse, was probably late 16th century, although there have been many later revisions and additions. It is said to be haunted by Sylvia, a woman murdered by her husband when she was caught with her lover, although there are no early records of hauntings and the tale is thought to stem from an urban myth around the time of the Second World War.*

Just opposite the Llindir Inn is a row of two-storey stone cottages (Henllan almshouses built in 1814).

From Henllan the route goes through woods and farmland, past historic ruins, to the outskirts of Denbigh with views to the castle and the Clwydian Hills beyond. It traverses the wooded Mount, quarried for castle building stone, to ascend the back streets of the walled town of Denbigh to the castle.

To continue the route from the five-road crossroads, turn left (east) along Denbigh Street (B5382) passing the bus stop opposite the community shop. *Note that there are no bus services from Henllan to Denbigh between 1330 and the last bus of the day at 1740.* Just before the school fork right up Ochr y Bryn and at the last houses on the right, take the path forking left over

The ruins of the 16th Century Foxhall Newydd

The North Wales Limestone Way

Bluebells in Coed Coppy

Primroses on the sunken bridleway leading to Lodge Farm

a stile (waymarked with Community Miles and Clwydian Way) into a field. Go alongside the fence on your left to reach a stone-slab stile in a limestone wall at the edge of a wood. Pass through this narrow wood via a waymarked wooden stile (in a limestone wall) leading into a field. Continue along the edge of the wood going past **Foxhall Newydd** (*name possibly from "Foulke's new hall"*) through the trees off to the right.

Foxhall Newydd was never finished and has been a ruin for over 150 years. Nevertheless it is a scheduled ancient monument and Grade I listed as a highly ambitious and accomplished late Elizabethan/early Jacobean large scale three-storey house, one of the most sophisticated of its date in Wales. It was begun in 1592 by John Panton, Recorder of Denbigh, but also Chief Secretary to the Lord Keeper, to show to his peers in his native Denbigh his new-found wealth and success.

Towards the end of the wood the path curves right, passes through a gate, then bears slightly left along the boundary wall of **Foxhall** and heading southeast. Where this wall curves left head across the field aiming for a marker post by a holly tree (medium size, distinctly smaller than all other visible trees).

Foxhall, not well seen from the path, is a Grade II* listed early Tudor gentry house, the ancient seat of the Lloyd family that provided High Sheriffs in the mid-sixteenth to eighteenth centuries. The most noteworthy of the Lloyds was Humphrey Llwyd (1527–1568) an important physician, map maker and antiquary regarded as one of the great Renaissance figures of Wales.

Go through a break in the wall ahead, then through a wooden gate to take the delightful wandering path through **Coed Coppy** with, in spring, masses of wild garlic, wood anemones and bluebells with glimpses of the golf course to your left.

The path exits the main wood through a wooden gate into sparser woodland and veers right to avoid the golf course track, then exits the trees over a stile into a field. Head diagonally across the field, aiming towards the Jubilee Tower on **Moel Famau** on the skyline, through a gate in the fence then continue to a steel gate in the field corner by a farm and a road; immediately turn back sharply right down a track heading west.

In 250 metres turn left down an

Denbigh Castle with the Clwydian Hills beyond

enclosed grassy bridleway, with masses of primroses in spring, to end at a gate/stile before **Lodge Farm**.

Lodge Farm is a large Grade II listed late 18th century farmhouse, possibly developed from an earlier building on the site.

Go through the farmyard, over a stile, keeping the hedge and copse on your left, to a stile leading to a surfaced lane. Turn right along the lane for 250 metres, with good views to Denbigh Castle and the Clwydian Hills beyond, turning right on the A543 and in 50 metres cross to a large lay-by.

The North Wales Limestone Way 53

The ruins of Denbigh Castle built on tilted limestone strata

Ruins of the triple-towered gatehouse to Denbigh Castle

At the top of the lay-by. go through a wide kissing gate with marked footpath sign to a well-surfaced path with views left over fields to Denbigh town. Just beyond a steel gate on the right there is an information board for Mount Wood; fork left, uphill here through the trees, with outcrops of bedded limestone in the bank where there is a small, old quarry. As you breast the top of the rise (Castle Mount or The **Mount**) and reach the edge of the wood there are superb views over to the **Castle** above the town of **Denbigh** and to the Clwydian hills beyond. The path is well-surfaced and supplied with seats and information boards. The path then descends into the wood, at first gradually, then more steeply as it bypasses an old quarry, to join a wider path at the base of the slope.

Turn sharply left, with houses to your right and the wood and quarry on your left. Exit the wood through an ornamental metal arch in the form of a branching tree in leaf to reach a kissing gate onto the road with signs pointing up the road on the right to the castle. Go up the pavement, looking down left to council offices, and up ahead

The North Wales Limestone Way

on the bluff to Denbigh Castle. At the T junction the pavement dies out, but go left up Love Lane towards the castle, past the castle lodge on the right to turn up right on Castle Lane (Lon Castell). As you ascend, the castle is closely above you and the foundations on limestone outcrops can be seen.

Fork right up Castle Hill, then in 20 metres turn right up steps to an open grassy area with the imposing triple-towered castle gatehouse in front of you. This completes Stage 3.

On a wall by the steps, facing a terrace of houses, is a plaque indicating that H. M. Stanley (1841–1904; the journalist and explorer) was born near here, the original house having been demolished.

Denbigh Castle *is a Grade I listed Scheduled Ancient Monument, an important example of a late 13th/early 14th century military architecture associated with Edward I's master mason/architect James of St. George. It was built by Edward de Lacy, Earl of Lincoln, under licence from Edward I, starting in 1282 with the first phase defining the boundary of the town (nowadays referred to as the upper town) complete by 1294. The most striking feature is the gatehouse which consists of three linked towers enclosing a central area. Originally the gate included a drawbridge and two portcullises with murder holes and arrow slits for defence. The castle is managed by CADW and is well worth an extended visit. Most of the town walls remain relatively intact together with one of the two gates and four towers. Access to the town walls requires a key from the castle custodian or from Denbigh Library.*

Denbigh *occupies a commanding position overlooking the Vale of Clwyd from its rocky hill. It may have had Iron Age ancestry and was certainly a base for the Welsh princes in the 13th century, although no trace of any such buildings has been found. The present town, developing from the castle as an English walled town in the 13th century, later spread downhill outside the walls. It retains many old buildings in addition to the castle and town walls.*

For shops, accommodation, refreshments and buses, turn left when facing the castle and head downhill with the imposing tower of St. Hilary's Chapel to the right.

What can be seen today is the surviving west tower of St. Hilary's Chapel, built c. 1300 within the walled upper town of Denbigh. After the construction of St. Mary's in 1874 the

Sign on the wall in front of Denbigh Castle

The Burgess Gate in the Denbigh town walls

chapel fell into disuse and, apart from the tower, was demolished in 1923.

At the next crossroads head straight across downhill on Castle Hill, past an early 19th century terrace constructed from stone plundered from the ruined castle, through the imposing gateway of Burgess Gate.

The Burgess Gate is a largely intact two-storey gatehouse, originally with portcullis, which controlled access between the upper town (and castle) and the lower town (and market place). An information board inside the gate provides details.

Head steeply downhill turning right on Broomhill Lane then via Temple Bar Square down on the left to arrive abruptly on the high street, with its numerous shops, places to eat and bus stops for express and local buses. Denbigh Library is at the right hand end of the main street.

The library building, originally the town hall (and County Hall), though altered in the 18th and 19th centuries, still retains much of its original 1572 structure. The ground floor would originally have been open for use as a market area, with the first floor supported by eight columns, seven of which can still be seen inside. The library is well worth investigating; it is a useful source of local information, maps and bus timetables and also holds keys to the town walls (*that can be borrowed for a small deposit; well worth the excursion*).

In front of the library is a bronze statue of Sir Henry Morton Stanley ("Doctor Livingstone I presume") with hand outstretched, and judging by the polish on the hand it has frequently been "shaken" by visitors. In 2020 there was a campaign to have the statue removed, as it was regarded in some quarters as an unacceptable face of colonialism (somewhat ironic as Denbigh Castle and walls were also a – much earlier – example of English colonialism).

The statue of Henry Morton Stanley in front of Denbigh Library ("Dr. Livingstone, I presume...")

Stage 4: Denbigh to Llanfair Dyffryn Clwyd

Start: Denbigh Castle
(SJ 01573 65859)

Finish: Village centre,
Llanfair Dyffryn Clwyd
(SJ 13408 55425)

Distance: 19.2km (11.9 miles)

Ascent: 416m (1363 feet)

Time: 5 hours 29 minutes

Stage Summary: Leave the castle through a gap in the walls and make a steep descent and circuit of wooded castle crags. Field paths and minor roads with some woodland are followed by a short section along a main road verge into Rhewl. A fine riverside stony track, then field paths lead into Ruthin centre. Streets and paths are taken through the outskirts, then field paths and minor roads through the vale to the finish. Incorporates two historic market towns with Norman castles.

Refreshment: There is plenty of choice in Denbigh and Ruthin. In between there is the historic Drovers Arms in Rhewl. In Llanfair DC the White Horse is open evenings and also weekend lunchtimes.

Transport: Arriva Bus Service 51 from Denbigh to Rhyl and Service 51 from Denbigh to Ruthin run hourly, passing through Rhewl. Service X51 (Ruthin – Wrexham) passes through LlanfairDC.

Accommodation: Ruthin Castle Hotel and The Castle Hotel, Ruthin are perhaps the best-known hotels, but there are other hotels, pubs and B&B's. Eyarth Station Guesthouse is on the route close to LlanfairDC.

As a Day Trip: Park in Denbigh at one of the council pay and display car parks (Factory Ward is handy). At the end of the stage take the X51 bus (Wrexham-Ruthin) from LlanfairDC (School stop) to Ruthin and the 51 (Ruthin-Denbigh) back to the start.

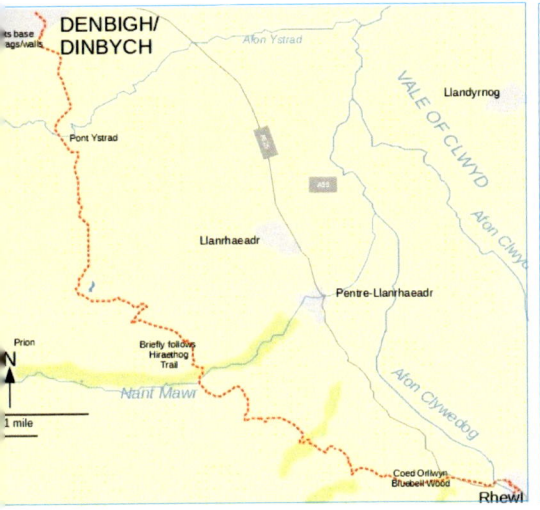 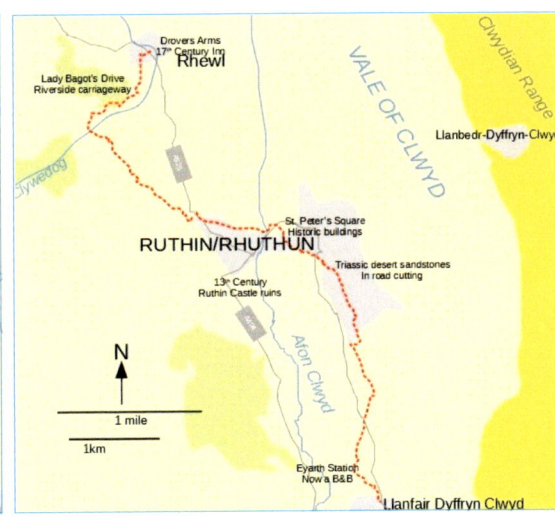

The walk

Between Denbigh and Ruthin the outcrop of the Carboniferous Limestone on this western side of the Vale of Clwyd is much broken up by faulting. The route therefore alternates between the limestone – which tends to be drier underfoot – and the wetter Silurian mudstones. Only towards Ruthin, where we dip into the Vale of Clwyd, do we move onto the brick-red Triassic sandstones. Initially we descend the Castle crags then traverse farmland via footpaths and minor roads to cross the river at the old bridge of Pont Ystrad. A section, predominantly on minor roads with views across the vale to the Clwydian Hills takes us down to the village of Rhewl and its historic pub.

Facing the triple-towered gatehouse, turn left on the track to a car park, then through a gate in the town walls, down steep stone steps, across the minor lane and through a gate to descend a zig-zagging path that levels out as it joins the perimeter path through the Castle Woods.

The North Wales Limestone Way

The limestone cliffs below Denbigh Castle

Turn right at the bottom along a prominent path which has iron railings on its left and limestone cliffs on the right, through the wood. Shortly the town walls can be seen on top of the cliffs and the path skirts the base of a part-ruined tower projecting from the walls. *This tower guards the castle well.*

As the path climbs, turn left down a path with a steel fence on the left and scrub on the right and pass from the Clwyd Limestones and Carboniferous Ffernant Formation underfoot to the Silurian mudstones. Go through a gate and take the waymarked, sometimes wet and muddy, path diagonally down and across a field, to the field corner on the right.

There are good views over to the Clwydian Hills, whilst looking back the castle and town walls are largely hidden by the woods. To the east are the fine college buildings known previously as Howell's School, which owes its origins to a bequest made by Thomas Howell who died in 1540; the school was not built until 1858–1859 and opened in 1860. The Grade II listed original building has been much extended, but retains a Tudor Gothic style and is of collegiate character. It was formerly a girls' boarding school but since 2015 has become the co-educational (boarding) Myddelton College.

Here, go through the kissing gate, alongside the hedge on your left, to the next field corner where a slate slab crosses a small stream. Go through several fields via kissing gates, keeping close to hedges, until the land drops away to the left revealing the sparsely wooded valley of the River Ystrad. Go over a wooden stile and contour round the top of the slope, then descend to a metalled road via a wooden stile.

Turn left down to the river which is crossed by an early 19th century single-arch bridge (**Pont Ystrad**) and head steeply uphill, past a turn to the right.

As the slope eases the house on the right, Fferm Llys, has a motte in the garden shown on the map, ideally placed for control of the river crossing below. The site, known as **Llys Gwenllian**, *according to Cadw, was a medieval motte and bailey associated with a daughter of Llewelyn ap Iorwerth. Little can be seen of it now from the road as the modern house and farm buildings obscure it.*

Go past the house and take the right hand road signposted Prion and Saron, with hedges on either side, going past footpath signs and the fine house of **Rosa Fawr**, *a substantial Georgian house incorporating medieval and 17th century fabric.* Take the minor road on the left, signposted Llanrhaeadr, passing Bryn Rossa (**Bryn Rosa** on the map) and Berlian Bach. Here take the bridle path heading uphill which soon turns into a path, bounded by holly trees and often a watercourse, on the slopes of **Bryn Mulan**. Occasional blocks of limestone indicate a return to the Clwyd Limestones underfoot and this continues to Rhewl. At the top of the slope there are fine views east over the Vale of Clwyd to the Clwydian Hills.

The path emerges onto the access drive for Bryn Derwen and goes along this to the road ahead. Turn left and in 25 paces take the footpath on the left over a wooden stile, going downhill between a line of old trees on the left and hedge on the right. In the bottom of the dip on the left there is the **Ty-mawr Reservoir**; go between two steel gates, over the stream on a bridge and cross a boggy section to a wooden stile. Continue in the same direction, uphill, ignoring the wooden stile on the right, and go along the hedge on the right, to a steel gate. Go through this, by the hedge on the

Looking across the Vale of Clwyd from Bryn Mulan

The North Wales Limestone Way

right, with the field sloping up on the left to the field corner and a stile. Once over this follow the hedge on the left to the next field corner and another stile. Carry on along the hedge on the left with **Rhewl Farm** below to the right. Over the next stile at a kink in the hedge is a cream painted house to the right. Head down to two stiles into a paddock then alongside the house boundary round to the right to another stile and the access drive to Ty Hen.

Turn left down the drive and in 20 paces turn right on the metalled road. Turn left at the next T junction then straight across at the crossroads.

Where the road takes a sharp turn to the left take the footpath to the right (marked Mynydd Hiraethog – the **Hiraethog Trail**, a 40 mile route across the Denbigh Moors). At first this is very wet – essentially a stream – then it goes through a wooden gate onto a leaf-floored track with overgrown hedges each side and, in twenty paces, over a wooden stile to continue on the sunken track which takes significant drainage from the fields either side. The flanking hedges are overgrown but the way eases as the track descends through a rock cutting (cleaved and jointed Silurian mudstones) and the stream disappears, but overgrown holly trees are still an issue. The track ends at the edge of **Fron-Parc Wood** where a railway sleeper footbridge gives access to a wooden stile and the wood beyond.

The main stream heads left along the wood boundary; a minor stream beyond it goes down a sunken track or gully. Our path heads half left between the two on a raised bank and curves slightly right, down through the trees, keeping the gully close on the right. A more obvious path joins from the left and this is taken down to a forestry track at the base of the slope.

*This wooded valley is the **Nant Mawr** and the river flows northeast through **Pentre Llanrheadr** to join the Afon Clywedog, which itself joins the River Clwyd near Denbigh. The **Coed Nant Mawr SSSI** is a 21.5 hectare (53 acre) site comprising woodland along both sides of this steeply incised valley. Our route cuts across the western end of the SSSI, the bulk of which lies downstream from the bridge. The wood is regarded as a large and particularly fine example of its type, with ash, wych elm and sessile oak. The majority of the wood lies on Silurian rocks, but to the east Carboniferous Limestone is present.*

Go left on the forestry track (waymarker post) – there are charcoal burners the other side – over the bridge across the rushing stream. Jump a side stream on the left to a sunken path, flanked by trees and ferns, steeply uphill along the left edge of the wood. At the top of the slope leave the wood through an iron gate onto a minor road and turn left (the Hiraethog Trail turns right). Just beyond the farm of **Pen-y-Waen**, *at the edge of the farmyard, there is a signed path heading southeast across a large field (crossed by a tree-flanked stream); this is passable in summer, but too boggy in winter so the preferred drier alternative is to use the road.*

Take the road round, passing **Talyrnau Farm** and a cottage (Talyrnau) on the left and turning right at the road junction to arrive at the other end of the wet path just below **Tan-yr-Accar**. Ignore the path marked to the left, but continue on this minor road, taking the left turn uphill at the Grade II listed Capel y Wern (*built 1860, since converted to residential use*). As the road levels off the views open up down to the Vale of Clwyd farmland and the hills beyond; this is a minor road with central grass strip, hedged with holly and hardly any traffic.

Continue past turns to the right and left, passing the large two storey house of **Bryn Eglur**, to descend past cottages on the right to enter a wooded valley (the Nant Goch) where the stream has cut deep into Silurian rocks producing a substantial cliff on the right bank. The road exits the wood, but continues with hedges either side, to pass a road junction on the left. At a little double bend the road turns left in front of **Ty Mawr**, a substantial three storey farmhouse with outbuildings, then continues to the wood of **Coed Duon** on the right. *Views to the southern Clwydian Hills open up; the land down to the left lies on*

On the minor road near Bryn Eglur

Carboniferous Limestone with that to the right on Silurian rocks.

Just at the edge of the wood on the right, turn left at the footpath sign (on pole) down between house (Coed Duon) and outbuildings, bearing half right around the last outbuilding to reach a wooden farm gate into a field. Go down the left edge, avoiding electric fence(s), curving rightwards to go through a steel gate onto a farm track. Turn right and in 10m pass through a farm gate to enter a field. Head diagonally right down the field to the angled corner (there is usually a small caravan here) against a coniferous wood.

Bluebells in the wood of Coed Orllwyn

Go through the steel gate and along the fenced edge of the wood on the right to a steel gate leading into the yard of a cottage (Nant Goch).

Bear right on the access track downhill passing **Bachymbyd Bach** Farm (with fine old outbuildings including a granary on the left), through two more steel gates and the entrance to the farmyard to reach a minor road at the end of the track. Go straight across the lane and over a wooden stile into a field with the traffic now visible on the main road below on the left. Head slightly right to the edge of the wood and along this to a wooden stile in the corner. Cross into the broadleaf wood (**Coed Orllwyn**; *known as a bluebell wood, but with a variety of other flowers, especially in spring*) and turn half left downhill on an obvious path through young trees to a wooden stile.

Climb over this to a farm track, turn right for five metres to a wooden stile in the hedge on the left giving access to the main road (A525 Denbigh o Ruthin). Turn right on the wide grass verge (carefully; busy, fast road) passing a lay-by just before the village sign for **Rhewl**.

Rhewl is a small village on the River Clywedog noted for its pub (The Drovers Arms), and start of Lady Bagot's Drive. It contains early 19th century houses, modern dwellings and, on the outskirts of the village, the former Rhewl railway station (now a private dwelling) on the Denbigh, Ruthin and Corwen railway – closed in 1965).

Continue along the verge into Rhewl, taking great care on the bridge across the Afon Clywedog. Just after the bus stop (express service 51 Denbigh-Ruthin), with the 17th century Drovers Arms beyond, take the metalled track and public footpath on the right signed Bontuchel.

To reach Ruthin we head along the delightful riverside track of Lady Bagot's Walk, then across fields to the outskirts of the town. A climb up into the centre allows us to examine the many fine old buildings, including the castle, before heading through streets and along the vale to reach the fine old limestone village of Llanfair Dyffryn Clwyd (known as LlanfairDC). A fine road cutting of Triassic dune-bedded red sandstone provides a geological diversion.

The next bit of the walk is along the delightful Lady Bagot's Drive; this was an Edwardian carriageway built by Lord Bagot for his wife to ride from Bontuchel to Rhewl along the scenic, often rocky, banks of the Afon Clywedog.

Cross the river on the, probably 17th century, packhorse-style stone bridge of **Rhyd-y-Cilgwyn** and bend left at the farm. Just past the houses on the right the track loses its metalling and runs alongside the river flanked by trees. Past the house and garage of Glan Clywedog the track enters woods and the river rushes, babbles and steepens over limestone bedrock.

The remains of a leat are soon visible on the nearside of the river (a sluice led to a flour mill at Rhyd-y-Cilgwyn) with limestone cliffs shortly appearing on both sides of the river. Shortly after well-preserved twin limekilns on the right of the

The River Clywedog from Lady Bagot's Drive

The North Wales Limestone Way

Twin limekilns next to Lady Bagot's Drive

track, turn left to cross the river via a footbridge with a modernised cottage almost at river level on the far side.

Take the slabbed path through a gate and take the path uphill with the cottage below on the right and a fern-adorned bank on the left. At a wooden summerhouse ahead turn sharp left, passing through iron gates to a track beyond. Pass a farmhouse and outbuildings on the left, taking the stony track rightwards to turn left at a metalled road, then right in a few metres over a wooden stile into fields.

Keep the hedge or line of trees on your left until the hedge angles rightwards at a slight dip when you cross a wooden stile left into the next field. Go along the field edge on the right with mature trees, sparse hedge and fence to another wooden stile in the field corner. Keep following field edges and stiles, passing the farm of **Ty'n-y-caeau** on the right until good views appear across the Vale of Clwyd to the Clwydian Hills with the Jubilee Tower of Moel Famau prominent. Ahead the tower of the modern Ruthin Castle is now visible. The way is often boggy, but with clear waymarkers; at one stage it crosses a farm access track to continue along field edges. At an obvious farm track cross the stile inset from the field edge, turn sharp left heading downhill with a fence on the left with mature trees flanking an almost dry gully. As you near **Ruthin** and its industrial outskirts the field slopes down more to the left and here the underlying geology changes from Carboniferous Limestone to the bright brick-red soils of the Early Triassic Kinnerton Sandstone. The easiest way down the field is to stay at the top of the bank heading towards an electricity pole, then down to cross a stile in the hedge with houses across the field straight ahead.

Turn sharp left along the stony track,

through steel gates to the main road. Turn right past the service station then cross the road at the Pelican Crossing to reach a multi-use track alongside the road passing the "Ruthin – Historic Market Town" sign. Turn left onto the surfaced footpath which skirts the newly built school to the left to go along sports pitches, with houses and hedges to the right, heading towards the tower and steeple of St. Peter's Church.

Ruthin *is a picturesque market town set in the southern Vale of Clwyd. It was formerly a Welsh settlement, but following years of turbulence was settled by the English when Edward I permitted the de Grey family to build a strong castle in 1282. It became a prosperous Anglo-Welsh market town centred on St. Peter's Square and today retains many fine historic buildings.*

Keep straight ahead past changing rooms and sports pitches to cross a footbridge over the river then bend half right to a kissing gate and the main road. Turn left along the pavement (passing a bus stop for X51 Wrexham– Ruthin – Denbigh – Rhyl continuation) taking the first turn right after Min-yr-Afon and heading rightwards uphill (on Prior Street) with the church above on the left. At the

St. Peter's Square – the centre of Ruthin

Maen Huail (Arthur's Stone) in Ruthin centre

top of the hill enter St. Peter's Square.

St. Peter's Church *is a Grade I listed collegiate and parish church, originally founded in 1310, and well worth a visit. The tower was altered and spire added in c.1859 and is now visible from miles around. It has extremely fine late medieval wood-panelled roofs amongst many other fine features, and provides a calm respite for a few minutes.*

The square has many features of interest; the old Courthouse, the Eyes of Ruthin, The Castle Hotel, the Castle Pharmacy and, outside Barclays Bank, King Arthur's Stone.

The ornate stone clock tower erected 1883 commemorates Joseph Peers who was Clerk of the Peace for the County of Denbigh for fifty years.

The Eyes of Ruthin are the multi-dormered tiled roof of the former Myddelton Arms which is now part of the Castle Hotel.

The Castle Hotel, formerly the White Lion, is an early 18th century (c.1730) three storey brick building originally owned by the Myddelton family of Ruthin Castle and now a hotel, restaurant and pub.

Maen Huail, also known as Arthur's Stone, is a large rough limestone block standing just outside Barclay's Bank. Tradition has it that on it King Arthur

The Old Court House, Ruthin centre

beheaded Huail, brother of Gildas the historian, although it is thought more probable that it was simply a preaching stone formerly set in the middle of the square.

The Castle Pharmacy (Boots) is supposedly the oldest building in Ruthin (2, Well Street) having survived destruction by Owain Glyndwr in 1400.

The Old Court House is a timber framed building of 1401, formerly the courthouse of the lordship of Ruthin, but now the National Westminster Bank. On the west gable end are the remains of a gibbet and the cells still exist below the beamed courtroom.

Nantclwyd House (Nantclwyd y Dre) on

Nantclwyd y Dre on Castle St., the earliest surviving timber-framed townhouse in Wales

Castle St. is a fine 16th century two storey timber-framed house with an earlier core of 1434–35. It is said to be the earliest timber-framed town house in Wales – well worth a look.

Continuing on Castle St. leads to **Ruthin Castle** *which was a large stone castle built from 1277 (by Dafydd, brother of Llewelyn ap Gruffydd) for Edward I in return for the treacherous help given to Edward in the invasion of North Wales that year. When developed, the moated castle had a central court defended by curtain walls and round wall towers with a twin-towered gatehouse to the southeast; the medieval town did not have town walls (unlike Denbigh). The castle fell into a state of disrepair and was sold to Sir Thomas Myddelton of Chirk, but in 1642 the English Civil War resulted in the castle being repaired at the Crown's expense and garrisoned against the Parliamentarians. During an eleven week siege the castle was bombarded by artillery and from 1648 the walls were torn down to prevent reoccupation by hostile forces. Stones from the castle were doubtless used in the town's buildings.*

The present-day Ruthin Castle Hotel dates from the mid 19th century when it was built – and rebuilt – in the original castle grounds as a private mansion in local red sandstone. In the 1960s the castle was purchased at auction and converted into a hotel – which it remains to the present day.

It is worth just popping in here to look at Ruthin Castle Hotel – built of local fine red sandstone – but more particularly at some of the remains of the original castle. Just before the gate, a mid-19th century construction of red and grey sandstone, a sign on the wall indicates the Cunning Green path. This leads between the walls of Ruthin Castle and those of the Lord's Garden and is probably the route that would have been taken by the medieval

The North Wales Limestone Way

occupants of Nantclwyd y Dre down to the river. Its name derives from Coney Green, an area where rabbits were kept.

To continue the route from St. Peter's Square, head down Well St., joining the A525 briefly, then along Llanrhydd Road (signposted "Hospital Ysbyty"). Pass the entrance to the hospital and prepare to turn right into Bryn Glas. A brief detour here is worthwhile. *Just past Bryn Glas, enter a deep, wooded road cutting with superb exposure of the dune-bedded red aeolian desert sandstones of the Early Triassic Kinnerton Sandstone, perhaps the best example in the Vale of Clwyd.*

Road cutting displaying dune-bedded desert sandstone on outskirts of Ruthin

Retrace your steps to Bryn Glas, turn left along the road and subsequent surfaced path, across Erw Goch and the continuation path to intersect Erw Goch again. Turn left, then right along Maes Cantaba, forking left where the road bends right, then in a few paces forking right along Bro Deg (taking the first Bro Deg at the bend in the road gets to the same path) then at the end of the road head half right across the grass to a signed footpath.

Go alongside the backs of houses into open fields with the Clwydian Hills on the skyline to the left. At the end of the first field turn sharp right along the hedge and at the next field boundary turn sharp left by **Cantaba Farm**.

Follow the fence or hedge across two fields to a minor road, then turn right for 50 paces, go through a farm gate on the left and head diagonally right across the field to a visible stile in the hedge. Climb the stile to join the A525, cross with care (sign for Eyarth Station B&B 600m) and take this quiet lane past the access to **Ffynogion** Farm to reach the Eyarth Station guest house.

Looking back to Eyarth Station from the maize field

19th Century almshouses and war memorial in Llanfair DC

Ffynogion is a large Grade II listed early 17th century gentry farm house, timber-framed originally, belonging to the Pryces of Ffynogion.

The guest house is the modified **Eyarth Station** which was active between 1864 and 1962, initially operated by the Denbigh, Ruthin and Corwen Railway later incorporated into the London and North West Railway. There were several trains a day passing through the station, which had waiting rooms at the north and south ends of the platform, and a small goods yard. Trains ran to Corwen and Chester. The Denbigh, Ruthin and Corwen railway was a standard gauge line that was closed in 1962; the track no longer exists, and the guesthouse is the best-preserved of the few buildings that remain.

Just before the old station (house) take the footpath on the left up the left edge of a field of maize and two smaller fields (the second of which now contains the Cae Mair housing development) to the road. Turn right and in 100 metres reach the end of the stage at the centre of **Llanfair Dyffryn Clwyd**.

Llanfair Dyffryn Clwyd is a small village on the A525 south of Ruthin in an elevated *position above the River Clwyd. It lies near the southern end of the Vale of Clwyd and, though it sits on the Kinnerton Sandstone, the older buildings are of Carboniferous Limestone. Several of the buildings in the older part of the village, which clustered around the church, are listed. Newer developments are to the west of the centre, towards the river. There is a war memorial, with almshouses behind, bus stop and, across the A525 road, the Grade II listed White Horse Inn and the Church of St. Cynfarch and St. Mary's (a double-aisle medieval building with some 15th century stained glass).*

Stage 5: Llanfair Dyffryn Clwyd to Maeshafn

Start:	Village centre, Llanfair Dyffryn Clwyd (SJ 13408 55425)
Finish:	Village green, Maeshafn (SJ 20206 60992)
Distance:	21.1km (13.1 miles)
Ascent:	707m (2321 feet)
Time:	6 hours 32 minutes

Stage Summary: Leaving the village, field paths lead to a steep climb through woods to a minor road, then a path across the Clwydian Hills. Descent on Offa's Dyke Path through farmland across the Alyn Valley and along the river to Llandegla. Field and woodland paths with open upland pasture, then through fields and lanes to Eryrys. An ascent of open pathways over Bryn Alyn with field and woodland paths to Maeshafn.

Refreshment: In Llanfair DC the White Horse is open evenings and also weekend lunchtimes. The Three Pigeons pub and restaurant is a kilometre off route in Graigfechan, then nothing until the community café and shop in Llandegla. There is some uncertainty about the Crown Hotel in Llandegla (Pen-y-Stryt). The community shop (and Raven Inn pub) in Llanarmon are 1.5km off route, The Rose and Crown, traditional pub/restaurant in Graianrhyd (open evenings and weekend lunchtimes) is 1km off route. The Sun Inn in Eryrys (open mid-afternoon and evenings) is on the route, as is The Miners Arms pub in Maeshafn. The Owain Glyndwr Inn at Gwernymynydd is about 1.5km along Ffordd Bryngwyn from Maeshafn (about halfway to Gwernymynydd).

Transport: Ruthin has an hourly express service to Denbigh (X51 then on to Rhyl 51) and Wrexham (X51 via Llandegla and LlanfairDC). Eryrys has a limited service to and from Ruthin and Mold (#2) (last service to Ruthin 1706, but not Saturday, to

The North Wales Limestone Way

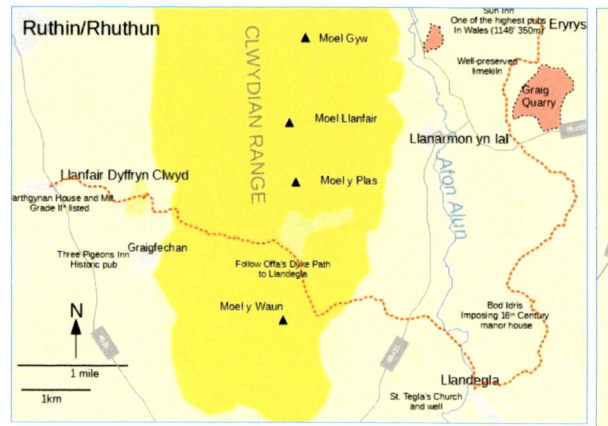

Mold 1611 schooldays only). Maeshafn has a 1700 bus to Ruthin, which has 0900 and 1050 buses to Maeshafn taking 40 minutes.

Accommodation: The Three Pigeons Inn in Graigfechan offers limited (usually only weekly) accommodation and camping, but is 1km off route, Bryn Dŵr Pods and B&B in Llandegla, the Llyn Rhys campsite is 0.5-1km off route south of Llandegla, Owl Lodge is 2km south of Llandegla, At the time of writing it is not clear if Bod Idris Hall is offering accommodation. Gweryd Lakes Fishing near Llanarmon yn Ial is 2km off route. The Raven Inn, Llanarmon yn Ial, a community pub with three self-catering rooms, is 1.5km off route. The Sun Inn, Eryrys has a 2 bedroom apartment over the pub let for short breaks and weekly on a self-catering basis. The Glan Llyn farmhouse (B&B and stabling for horses) 1.5km north of Eryrys, is virtually on the route, just east of Burley Hill Quarry. Hafan Deg B&B, is in Maeshafn (01352 810465). The Maeshafn Youth Hostel is no longer operative. There are various places in Ruthin accessible by bus.

As a Day Trip: Park at one of the riverside car parks in Ruthin. Take the X51 bus to LlanfairDC. When the stage ends in Maeshafn there is a bus back to Ruthin at 1700, taking 40 minutes. With two cars park one in LlanfairDC and one in Maeshafn village centre (limited parking in each case).

Consider parking a car in Maeshafn, taking the 0855 or 1155 bus (#2) from Maeshafn Tan y Graig bus stop arriving Ruthin/Market Street 0929 or 1229. Get the bus to LlanfairDC (X51 leaves Ruthin War memorial at 0931, 1031, 1131 etc.). Walk the route back to the car at Maeshafn.

The walk

Initially head across farmland to the edge of the vale. Climb steeply up the wooded scarp of the bounding faults to the open country of the uplifted Silurian Clwydian Hills. Cross these on a low pass to join the Offa's Dyke Path and descend the eastern slopes into the Alyn Valley with its flat-lying limestone beds. Head southeast along the river to Llandegla then turn north onto the Northeast Wales limestone plateau through farmland and high pasture to the village of Eryrys.

From the village centre head southeast on the main road and in a few metres take the road on the left signposted Graigfechan. Go down between houses until a stile on the right gives access to a permissive path across a field with a football pitch (which may be grazed by cows and sheep). Go half left to clip the corner of the pitch and head for a steel gate at the field corner. Turn left through the gate, heading up the edge of the field with hedge on your left. At the top of the field go over a stile and up the stony track bending right between farm buildings.

*The magnificent farm of **Garthgynan** is a Grade II* listed late 18th to early 19th century three storey stone and brick house with an earlier 17th century double pile house behind. There is a well-preserved small 17th century walled garden and a fine four-bay carriage barn. Many outbuildings are also Grade II listed.*

Once through the farm buildings the track becomes grassy and heads downhill. High up to the left is a limestone escarpment above extensive woods. At the bottom of the hill, the path takes a curve left to cross a stream; on the right is a large three storey building – **Garthgynan Mill** (***Melin Garth-gynan***) – *half in brick, half in stone – which is a Grade II* listed late eighteenth or early 19th century water mill used initially for grinding corn and later – with turbine installed – for supplying electricity to the farm's outbuildings.*

The path heads left uphill through a steel gate with stream on the left up a grassy hedged track to a wide wooden gate and stile over which is the B5429 road. Across the road there is another wooden gate structure with a wood behind and, a few metres to the right at a footpath sign, a stone stile with a substantial limestone slab cross-piece. Climb over this and take the obvious path uphill through the wood (**Coed Henblas**), slightly rightwards. There are waymarkers all through the wood.

You are now climbing the steep scarp of the eastern edge of the Vale of Clwyd, defined by the north-south Vale of Clwyd fault.

The path steepens as you ascend, with a couple of stepped sections. These lead to a limestone wall with another limestone slab stile. Over this to the left is an open field and footpath, to the right a wide path or track down to the North Wales Wildlife Trust's Graig Wyllt Nature Reserve,

Garthgynan

Garthgynan Mill

Graigfechan village and the Three Pigeons Inn, and straight ahead a less worn path steeply uphill.

*The North Wales Wildlife Trust's **Graig Wyllt** Nature reserve is in a wooded old limestone quarry on a steep hillside. It comprises deciduous woodland, sheltered scrubby areas, grassland and natural rock garden. There is an information board at the end of the track just beyond an old limekiln.*

*The village of **Graigfechan**, at the end of the track, contains The Three Pigeons Inn (a pub/restaurant); the current inn was rebuilt in 1777 on the site of a 12th century drovers' alehouse. It is said to be haunted.*

Take the path straight ahead steeply uphill through the wood and at a path junction keep uphill to the right; there are several lesser paths off to the right.

At the top the path briefly heads steeply down with open fields ahead, then bends right along the edge of the wood. Go over a stile into the field and head uphill along the field edge. *There are good views ahead to the Clwydian Hills with the noticeable change in vegetation from grassed fields below to open bracken and heather-covered hillside above.*

The underlying geology has now changed from Carboniferous Limestone to Silurian mudstones, something we'll be on until descending towards Llandegla.

Halfway up the field take the waymarked stile on the right and turn left up the next field. At the top of the field, cross the stile and go through a short scrubby section to reach the lane. Turn right up the lane, ignoring in 50 metres a footpath off to the left as the lane bends to the right. Continue along the lane, going past the house **Graig** and the lane that heads down right to Graigfechan. Climb the nicely graded lane (signed Llanarmon en Ial 5 miles) gently uphill until you reach a hairpin bend. Beyond the bridge take the path uphill through sheep-grazed rough pasture and head up the valley of **Boncyn y Waen-grogen** gradually moving higher above the stream heading towards a transmitter mast on the skyline. The path crosses several fence lines and, towards the top, a stile.

*Two diversions are feasible from here; a path diverts right and leads, somewhat uncertainly, to the summit of **Moel y Gelli** (361m, 1184 ft.) which has good views all round. To the south the last of the Clwydian Hills, Llantysilio Mountain and Llandegla Forest, then the Cambrian mountains, to the* *west in the distance Snowdonia, to the north the higher Clwydian Hills and to the east an extensive wood (**Nurse Fawr** – mixed conifers). A second diversion leads to the transmitter mast and buildings which give some shelter in windy conditions.*

In either case head east to the forest to join the Offa's Dyke Path going downhill south along the edge of the wood, taking a stony track via a stile and steel gate to a lane. Take this southwards, passing the small wood of **Nurse Gorlan** on the left, uphill then down for 0.7km, taking the waymarked Offa's Dyke Path over a stile on the left. The waymarked path passes **Tyddyn tlodion** and through fields, tracks and along streams, gently descending and passing from Silurian mudstones to the flat-lying strata of Carboniferous Limestone, across the flat floor of the Alyn Valley to cross the B5431.

Go through a gate to a grassy path with hedges and limestone ridges either side then after the next gate the path bears half right alongside a tree-lined bank. Go past a large block of limestone and turn sharp left at a fence and in 20 metres go through a wooden gate, turn right with a fence, trees and small stream on the right to a wide stream flowing fast towards you on the left. As the stream bends left, the path heads straight on to a footbridge with gates either end. Go along the edge of the field with small trees and stream backwater on the right and a conifer wood to the left.

Follow the edge of the plantation and at the far side go through a gate then straight on. Keeping the fence and trees on the right climb slightly through a gate, turn right then sharp left and down an avenue of trees with a pond on the right. Return to the fence on the left, crossing the stream by a wooden footbridge; turn right with

Looking north on Offa's Dyke Path, Nurse Fawr on right

stream and path on the right. Go past a little wood on the right in between branches of the stream which moves away from the path. The path climbs slightly uphill through a kissing gate and heads up the slope into the village of **Llandegla** with the old rectory on the left and church on the right.

The route turns sharp left just past the old rectory, but it is worth continuing into Llandegla, to visit the church and the community shop and cafe just down the road from the bus stop and car park. Much of the older part of the village was owned by the Bod Idris Estate. Llandegla is located on one of the main drover's roads from the northwest coast of Wales to the markets in England. The village and its inns benefitted from the trade, but by the late 19th century, with the development of railways, the trade tailed off. Quarrying became more important, but nowadays tourism is the main "industry".

St. Tegla's Church was completely rebuilt in 1866, although research suggests the original church was built around 1277. It retains an earlier font and outstanding medieval (probably 16th century) brass chandelier.

St. Tegla's Well, *a spring with reputed medicinal properties (particularly for curing epilepsy though involving a complex procedure with a cock and overnight stay in the church), rises on the left bank of the River Alyn, in a stone chamber about 100m south of the church and signposted with an information board.*

Just past the old rectory on the left and the church on the right take a sharp left turn along a metalled lane past houses, and on a bend in the lane across a wooden stile on the right into a field and aim half left to the far left corner of a wooded slope. Negotiate a series of wooden stiles, gates and foot bridges over streams with Community Miles waymarkers, bear left along the base of a steep wooded slope on the right. There is a large pond on the left. Follow the waymarkers, stiles and footbridge, occasionally with a Clwydian Way marker, with a fence on the left and sparsely wooded slope on the right.

At a waymarker go diagonally up the steep slope, and away from the fence, to a kissing gate in the fence at the top of the slope just before **Pen-y-Bryn Farm**. Join a stony track moving round the farm buildings on the left to the base of a set of stone steps up to the farmhouse. Here head between the farm and detached garages on a grassy track with waymarker through a steel gate into an orchard. Go alongside the hedge on the left to a kissing gate then between two fences along the top of a slope with limestone outcrop up on the right. Follow the fence to a steel gate via a waymarker below the limestone outcrop to a kissing gate in the fence.

Head diagonally right across the field to another kissing gate then across the next field to another kissing gate to the left of a farm gate to join a metalled lane on the bend. Head uphill on the lane, the access drive to **Bod Idris**, along an avenue of trees, through the fancy gateposts over a cattle grid, with a large ornamental pond to the right, turning left in front of an old stone barn.

Bod Idris *is an imposing Grade II* late Elizabethan (16th century) stone-built manor house with stone outbuildings (converted to accommodation). It has been a private residence, then a hotel, but is now believed to have become a private residence again.*

The path has recently been diverted left around the house, though older maps may show it circling right. Take the track round the left corner of the barn heading uphill through a steel gate round the back of the house with fine views down to the house, pond and hills beyond. At a muddy crossroad of tracks turn left into the wood, descending past a small stone building on the right then ascending through the wood with mostly conifers on the right and broadleaved trees on the left.

Just before a farm gate turn left through a gate bearing right round a hill on the left to a field corner. Take the track to the right below a ridge with, at the top of the slope, fine views across to the Clwydian Hills. Keep bearing right between limestone ridges on a faint grassy path to a gate at the edge of the field into a small

The 16th Century Bod Idris manor house

coppice, half right, meandering to another gate into a field.

Continue in the same direction with coppice on the left (in which there are old shafts from the early 19th century Allt Gymbyd lead mine), heading right of a large isolated tree into a broader field. Cross the rather wet field to the far right corner to a gate where the stream and trees on the stream banks juts into the field. Go over the stream via a drainage pipe bridge to a second gate then bear half right to a further gate. Turn left along the hedge with its fine old trees, through the wet field to a gate onto a metalled lane.

Turn right uphill with mature hedge on the left and wall on the right, passing two metal gates on the left to reach a footpath sign on the left. Climb steps up the bank and over the wooden stile into a field, then bear left and contour round the base of a steep gorse-covered ridge bearing left to a wooden stile over a very thick, slightly tumbledown, wall into boggy rough pasture. Go alongside the hedge on the right across tussocky, reedy and often watery pasture to reach a wooden stile leading to a metalled road.

The best way is to turn left on the road then pass the turn off on the left to reach a signposted footpath on the left. This position can also be reached via two footpaths, thus avoiding the road, but the first is extremely wet (the map shows it crossing a stream) and the road is the better option.

There are two paths signed over the stile; take the right hand (more northwesterly) one heading uphill slightly to the left of the little rise on the skyline. Continue in the same direction through an old field boundary to a wooden stile in a fence with scrub around and a couple of old shafts. Turn left along the left hand field boundary through scattered trees with, far to the right, **Graig Quarry**, then over a wooden stile in the next field corner with a shaft over the fence on the left.

There were two mines in the vicinity; the Creigiog (lead/silver/zinc) and the Maes-y-Pwll (lead) both worked east-west veins in the 19th century with several shafts and spoil heaps still evident.

Continue alongside the left hand hedge/fence and at a field gate angle away slightly right uphill towards a couple of stand-alone trees, through another open field boundary marked by a line of trees on a ridge, descending northwestwards through a coppice to join, at the bottom of the slope, a track contouring the wooded slope with a farm to the left.

The path through the field is not easy to follow, but the contouring track will be intersected at some stage. Turn right on the track until a white cottage (with solar panels) appears ahead where you turn left to a wooden stile with waymarker and descend the wooden steps (with wooden handrail). Go through a belt of trees and scrub and turn right on the road at the footpath sign.

Head down the road through fields and belts of trees, going straight across at the crossroads. The next section on open access land is a wonderful airy walk across upland pasture of the **Graig-Llanarmon yn Ial SSSI** with fine views to the west.

The 22.1 hectare (55 acre) site is a steep west-facing escarpment to the east of Llanarmon-yn-Ial, backed by the large Graig Quarry. It is of special interest for its limestone and acid grasslands and the transitions between the two. Many of the special plants are grasses, but perhaps of more interest to the non-specialist are plants such as the common rock rose, small scabious, wild thyme and salad burnet. Uncommon species include frog orchid, adder's tongue and moonwort.

Head steeply up a track and where the access drive to Pen Llwyn bends left, fork right up a path over a wooden stile into open country with the Clwydian Hills ahead across the Alyn Valley. The path initially hugs a newly rebuilt drystone wall on the right, where blackthorn scrub has been cleared, and skirts the huge hidden disused **Graig Quarry** on the right. Climb steadily past numerous limestone outcrops in an open airy position for about one kilometre.

*To the left, down in the valley is **Llanarmon yn Ial** and the disused **Pystyll Gwyn** limestone quarry and beyond these, on the skyline is Moel Famau with its Jubilee Tower. Further right is the limestone peak of **Bryn Alyn**.* An old drystone wall descends to meet our path as we descend through patches of gorse and blackthorn, between dipping limestone ridges, almost a dry valley. It descends through gorse patches to a wooden stile (Clwydian Way marker) with ferns in the limestone wall, to a road with a house over to the right, and a postbox just uphill. Turn right up the road, steeply, and turn right on the bridleway,

The Sun Inn, Eryrys, one of the highest pubs in Wales

passing a well-preserved limekiln on the right just before a house on the left.

Continue for 100m until a wooden stile on the left gives access to a footpath in the field keeping a fence and tumbledown wall on the right, heading uphill through upland pasture. There are several cross-walls though usually are crossed without the need for a stile, but keep the fence on your right. Where the path descends to a prominent line of trees go over the stile in the field corner and where the path veers to the right in a few metres go through a stile in the wall then along the wall, then fence, on your left down the field and through a farm gate to the road.

Turn left along the road to the crossroads in **Eryrys** with the church of St. David's on the left, the old village pump (which served the village for 50 years until 1987) on the right and the Sun Inn diagonally across.

***Eryrys** is one of the highest villages in Wales. Nowadays it is a sheep-farming area, but it used to be a centre for lead mining and quarrying.*

St. David's Church was built 1862-63, but closed to worship in the 1980s and is now a community centre.

The Sun Inn is an old inn shown on the first edition OS maps; it currently serves meals and real ales and has a two-bedroom apartment upstairs. It is one of the highest pubs in Wales at 1148 feet (350m) above sea level.

After examining a huge glacial erratic, climb up the open eastern slopes of Bryn Alyn with a brief diversion to one of its summits for the fine views, limestone pavement and relics of lead mining to descend via woods and farmland to the old mining village of Maeshafn.

Maen Digychwyn ("The Great Immovable Stone") a very large glacial erratic in Eryrys

The Eryrys Four Poster, a Bronze Age group of upright stones

Take the road signposted Mold at the crossroads, heading out of the village for 100m. Just before the first buildings on the left take the footpath on the left leading to Maen Digychwyn ("The Great Immovable Stone").

This is a very large glacial erratic. It now forms part of a garden wall, but was transported from the Ordovician rhyolites of Arenig Fawr during the last Ice Age some 14000 years ago and dumped here 30 miles to the east northeast when the glaciers melted.

Take the path heading west across the field, via a couple of stiles, to join the road Cae'r Odyn and turn right (*you could get here directly from the village if you want to bypass the glacial erratic*). Pass spoil heaps on the left and a Welsh Water treatment works on the right then, past all buildings, take a footpath on the right steeply uphill through pasture with limestone outcrops and a fine old drystone wall on the left. The path angles slightly rightwards with dipping limestone outcrops to the left, through pasture land with bracken and gorse. Cross another wall by ladder stile and head half left, meandering uphill through more gorse to a wooden stile over

The craggy west face of Bryn Alyn

Extensive limestone pavement on Bryn Alyn

Limestone landscape scarred by lead mining, eastern slopes of Bryn Alyn

a crossing wall. The path now levels out; the main route continues ahead to meet an old mine track, but if you want to climb one of Bryn Alyn's peaks (recommended) take the prominent green track left winding uphill to the **Bryn Alyn** access point.

About 50m south of the access point is the **Eryrys Four Poster**, *a group of four upright stones or slabs arranged at the inter-cardinal points (NE, SE, SW, NW) believed to be Bronze Age.*

Bryn Alyn has several subsidiary peaks, each just over 400m high, and each with superb all-round views from the peaks of Snowdonia to the northern hills and the sea. In addition there is a large area of limestone pavement, probably the most extensive in North Wales, on the eastern slopes.

The **Bryn Alyn SSSI** *covers 143.2 hectares (354 acres) encompassing the peak of Bryn Alyn and extending north and northwest from the village of Eryrys. It is of special interest for its range of limestone grassland, dry heath and the transitions from limestone to neutral and acidic grassland. In addition to rock outcrops, limestone ridges and sheer cliff faces there are areas of limestone pavement with specialist floral assemblages. There is birch-dominated* *woodland on the northern flank of the site.*

Between the green track and the mine track are numerous shafts, spoil heaps and scant remains of buildings from the lead mining past.

Follow the old mine track (*that ran from Pen-y-coed Farm to the Belgrave Mine and westwards down to the Alyn Valley*) to a clump of hawthorn trees and remains of old walls. *These are the remains of the engine house of the 19th century Belgrave Mine which worked an east-west vein of lead and silver.* Fork right away from the track and continue northwards to a stile that crosses the wall descending from the Bryn Alyn col.

Far ahead is the scar of the large **Burley Hill Quarry** and beyond it woods and further north, the sea. Bear slightly right downhill on a wide grassy path with bracken all round and descend through mine workings to reach a stile and the metalled road. Cross the road to a footpath, with farm access track and industrial buildings to the right.

The Burley Hill Quarry, a huge hole in the hillside, has been worked since the 19th century and at peak production had up to 300 lorries a day visiting the site with 800,000 tonnes of limestone produced. An application to extend the site in 2001 was rejected and the site is now closed.

It is quite common to see in the skies here the huge transport aircraft, the Airbus Beluga, which take aeroplane wings from the Broughton site. The planes appear to fly quite low, but are not particularly noisy – an amazing sight.

Go over the wooden stile, with waymarker for the Clwydian Way, meandering uphill through shafts (from the 1849–1891 lead/silver/zinc Pant Du Mine) and brambles to cross a short ladder

The abandoned Burley Hill Quarry from the northern slopes of Bryn Alyn

stile over a wall on the left, then turn right on a rough rocky path alongside the wall. There is scrub on the bank to the left and a field over the wall to the right. At the next corner go past the white cottage on the right, and continue northwards. *It is possible, following the Clwydian Way, to continue up the field, through a narrower muddy section to eventually bear left through a wooded col to more open fields beyond and aim for a derelict cottage and pond.*

The better route is to bear left and through a gap in the hedge to pass round a steep, partly wooded hill on the right and on round the side of the hill on a well-worn path, swinging right to avoid the deep quarry ahead. The path now goes alongside the quarry fence over wooden stiles, with a steep wooded bank on the left and open fields on the right. Go up to a slight col where the field narrows and descend towards an abandoned cottage on the left with pond in front of it. Now follow the edge of a wooded slope on the right, crossing a stile, turning sharp left to another stile immediately, then turn right and along the hedge on the right towards a cottage ahead. Join the access drive to the cottage and go past further cottages to the Miners Arms pub on the left, then on to the **Maeshafn** village green at the end of the stage.

__Maeshafn__ is a small village, mainly of limestone-built houses, which was a centre for lead mining. It was named after the Maes-y-safn Mine which extended eastwards from the __Afon Alun__, under the village as far as __Moel Findeg__. The village expanded during the 19th century, but contracted as mining finished in the early 20th century. The Methodist chapel, just off the village green, was built in 1820, enlarged in 1843 and rebuilt in 1863 as the population increased. It was finally rebuilt in

The 17th Century Miners Arms pub in Maeshafn

1900. Quarrying has also been important for the village, but the two large quarries nearby, Burley Hill and Aberduna, have now closed.

The Miners Arms pub was built in the 17th century as the village expanded in line with the development of lead mining; indeed it was originally the miners' pay office.

The former Maeshafn Youth Hostel was the first purpose-built hostel for the YHA, opening in July 1931 and designed by Sir Clough Williams Ellis (more famous for creating Portmeirion). It is now a private dwelling a few hundred metres southeast of the village centre on Ffordd Maeshafn.

Stage 6: Maeshafn to Brynford

Start:	Village green, Maeshafn (SJ 20206 60992)
Finish:	Crooked Horn Inn, Brynford (SJ 18657 74073)
Distance:	18.2km (11.3 miles)
Ascent:	595m (1952 feet)
Time:	5 hours 32 minutes

Stage Summary: Field and woodland paths to Loggerheads where the famous Leete Path runs alongside the River Alyn before traversing its cliffs. Descent to the next valley is followed by more woodland and field paths, with minor roads to another valley at Hendre then ascending similarly to the open access land on the edges of Halkyn Mountain where the scars of lead mining and quarrying are everywhere to be seen. After crossing the open Holywell Common the stage ends at an 18th century inn.

Refreshment: Miners Arms, Maeshafn (pub, restaurant) 01352 810464
Caffi Florence, Loggerheads Country Park 01352 810397
Crown Inn Pantymwyn (pub, restaurant, B&B) 01352 740462, 1km off route
White Horse Inn, Cilcain (pub, restaurant, B&B) 01352 740142, 1km off route
Y Dderwen (The Oak), Hendre 01352 741537, 0.8km off route.
Bluebell Inn, Halkyn 01352 780309, 2km off route east of Rhes y Cae
The Crooked Horn Inn (pub and restaurant) Brynford 07591 626673

Transport: Ruthin has 0900 and 1050 buses to Maeshafn taking 40 minutes.
Ruthin – Mold (and on to Chester) X1 and 1 services pass through Loggerheads. Service 14C Mold – Holywell, operated by P & O Lloyd (stopping at Brynford crossroads) has several buses a day. Service 14 (Mold-Denbigh, approximately 2 hourly) passes through Hendre.
Service 22A has hourly services From Brynford to Holywell (last service 1646)

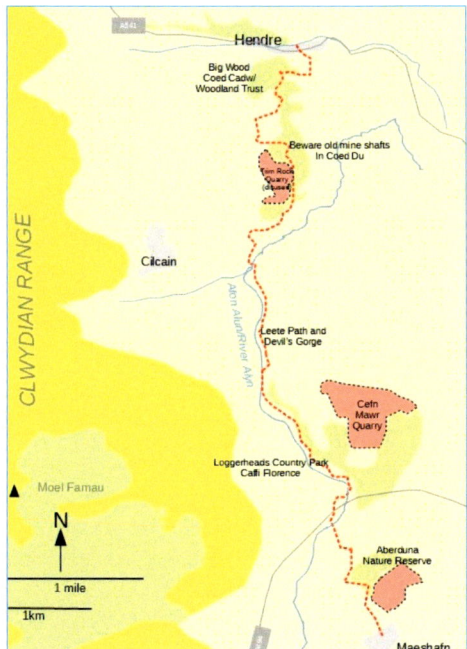

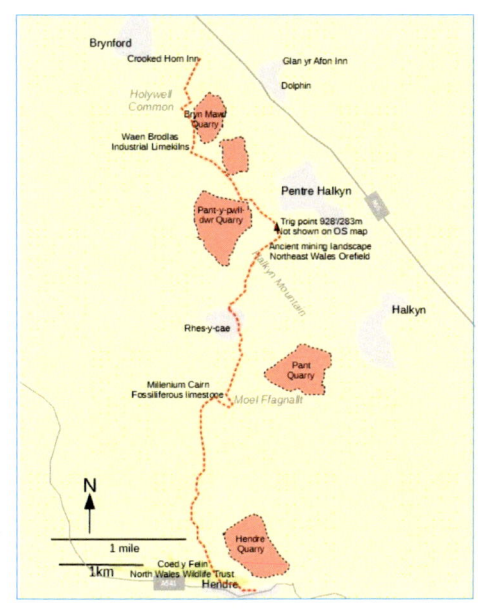

and from Holywell to Brynford 0837 hourly to 1722.

Service 126 (Holywell-Halkyn-Mold) has an hourly service calling at Pentre Halkyn PO and Halkyn Library).

Service 127 (Mold-Holway) passes through Brynford, but schooldays only, one per day each way.

Accommodation: We Three Loggerheads, Loggerheads nr. Mold (pub, restaurant, B&B) (01352 810337)

Crown Inn Pantymwyn (pub, restaurant, B&B) 01352 740462, 1km off route

Springfield Hotel and Health Club, Pentre Halkyn 0203 0248216, 1.2km from trig point on Halkyn Mountain

The Glan Yr Afon Inn, Dolphin, Milwr (pub, restaurant, B&B) 01352 710052, 1km walk from end of stage

The North Wales Limestone Way 91

Britannia Inn, Pentre Rd., Halkyn 01352 781564, 2km east of Rhes-y-cae off route
Travelodge, Halkyn 08719 846078, 3km off route
Midlist Farm B&B at Halkyn is 3km east of the route

As a Day Trip: Buses are scarce at both ends of the stage so using two cars is an easier option. Parking is easy in Brynford (opposite the Crooked Horn Inn).

The walk

Descend through woods via a nature reserve in a reclaimed quarry to the riverside limestone gorge at Loggerheads. Follow the famous Leete Path, traversing the cliffs high above the river to descend to the bridge at Cilcain.

With your back to the Miners Arms and the chapel off to the left, head uphill on the stony track between houses, past the village notice board and over a ladder stile.

(To go directly to the viewpoint, go straight ahead along the edge of the field, through a farm gate at the end, then halfway along the next field reaching a kissing gate on the right. Here the alternative way from the main route joins from across the field).

Go diagonally left on a hedge-lined stony bridleway, soon between drystone walls.

At a marker post with a viewpoint signed off right, the route goes straight on, but it is well worth taking a short detour to see into the quarry. *The* **Aberduna Quarry** *is now closed and is undergoing site restoration to provide upland ash woodland, calcareous grassland, scrub woodland and ponds to encourage bats, great crested newts, common lizards, adders, songbirds and butterflies.*

For the diversion take a vague path down and across the field, through the kissing gate

Maeshafn village centre with phone box (defibrillator) and chapel

and turn left along a wandering path which soon heads uphill and arrives at a viewing platform, benches and information board overlooking the quarry.

To return to the main route, retrace your steps across the field via a gap in the hedge to the marker post and turn right. Follow the main route between drystone walls, through a kissing gate and take the path, signposted Loggerheads, across and down a stone-studded field along a fence on the left to a kissing gate (*with information board for Aberduna Nature Reserve*).

The North Wales Wildlife Trust's **Aberduna Nature Reserve** *is an 8.7 hectare (21.5 acre) site of species-rich grassland and woodland looking west to the Clwydian Range and partly enclosing the old Aberduna Quarry. Lime-loving plants (including in spring bluebells, orchids, cowslips, rock-rose and moonwort) are widespread and provide food for the caterpillars of numerous butterflies. Twenty species of trees grow here.*

Go through the kissing gate and head downhill on a well-used path through open grassland and bracken, turning sharp right at a marked path junction. Take the now level path through bracken with scattered trees, particularly silver birch, and

Bridleway out of Maeshafn

The abandoned Aberduna Quarry, now a nature reserve

The North Wales Limestone Way

Moel Famau seen from a clearing in the woods

Descent on the bridleway to Loggerheads

occasional clear grass spaces which give fine views west to Moel Famau.

Continue into more trees and bracken, through an ivy-encrusted kissing gate and descending into the wood. The path is stepped and winds steeply down, turning right at a path junction then left at an old drystone wall, descending steeply with high steel fencing on the right to join the main path with the NWWT **Aberduna Nature Reserve** information board on the left.

A bridleway heads straight down over a wooden bar stile, but take the gravelly path to the right alongside high steel fencing around the edge of the **Coed y Fedw** with outdoor activity equipment visible through the trees. *The Coed y Fedw lead mine (1881–1884) old shafts can still be seen in the wood.* At the wood corner the waymarked path goes through a kissing gate into fields and alongside the hedge on the right, turning right at the fence corner. Here, by a group of large trees, you can look across the field to a prominent steel gate to the left of which is a kissing gate that you will shortly go through.

The public footpath takes a more circuitous route along the fence down to a

We Three Loggerheads Pub

Entrance to Loggerheads Country Park

finger post pointing left for Llanferres and right for Loggerheads.

Far ahead is the white building of Colomendy Hall; the collection of four-storey buildings to the right, forming part of the Colomendy site, is the Glan Alyn boarding school which was set up on site in 1969, but closed in the 1990s. **Colomendy** *itself was set up in 1939–40 as a wartime evacuation centre for children from Liverpool, built as two camps of red cedar huts. At the end of the war the camps were changed to educational establishments to give Liverpool children a taste of the countryside and the health benefits of being away from the city. The camp evolved into a site for shorter visits and over the years over 350,000 children have visited. In 1957 Liverpool Corporation purchased the site outright, but by 2005 they signed a 30 year deal with educational activity company Kingswood to redevelop the site as an outdoor pursuits centre.*

Take the path left and along the fence at the bottom edge of the field to reach the steel gate and then the kissing gate. Pass through the latter and turn right (to Loggerheads) on a tree-lined bridleway.

Continue downhill, swinging right at the bottom and over a humped wooden footbridge across the Afon Alun to arrive

The North Wales Limestone Way

at the main road with a filling station and Spar shop opposite. Turn right on the pavement across the road and the Loggerheads Weir on the right. The Three Loggerheads pub is on the right of the road.

"The Loggs" is a restored 17th century coaching inn with a traditional bar, vaulted restaurant and two B&B rooms. It is open 12 noon till late seven days a week.

Turn left at the Loggerheads Park sign and head into the car park. The park's buildings are off to the right.

The **Loggerheads Country Park** *is now managed by Denbighshire County Council. It was originally set up as tearooms by the Crosville Motor Company who ran popular bus tours here from Liverpool until the 1970s. The site is a spectacular setting in a wooded gorge with steep cliffs to the east on the banks of the River Alyn which commonly disappears underground in summer. It is worth spending some time looking round the various buildings here; there's a visitor centre with informative displays, shop, Cafe Florence and Pentre Water Mill.*

Much of this section of the walk falls within the **Alyn Valley Woods and Alyn Gorge Caves SSSI** *which covers 190.3 hectares (470 acres) along the steep limestone escarpment and wooded valley and gorge of the Afon Alun and subsidiary wooded valleys, together with the flatter valley bottoms. The site is noteworthy for the geology of the cave systems, many of which have a partial mining history, the botany of the deciduous woodland and grasslands and the grizzled skipper butterfly. The extensive mining of lead/zinc ores has locally modified the otherwise natural limestone soils; the nationally scarce spring sandwort, for instance, is found on old spoil heaps.*

The valley woodlands, stretching from just south of Loggerheads, north to Nant Alyn are

Following the Afon Alun through the limestone gorge

designated a Special Area of Conservation on three counts: alder woodlands on floodplains, mixed woodland on lime-rich soils associated with rocky slopes, and dry grasslands and scrublands on chalk or limestone. The locally uncommon wayfaring tree Viburnum lantana is present here in numbers, though at its northern limit in western Britain.

From the centre take a stone footbridge over the river to find a signpost for the Leete Path and follow it left, signed Devil's Gorge, on a wide gravel path at the base of the cliffs through the wooded gorge, initially at river level.

The Leete is a watercourse built in the 1820's from Loggerheads to Penyfron Mine (lead, silver and zinc) at Nant Alyn, a few kilometres north of Loggerheads. It is now disused, being largely filled in, but was an important way of getting water to the water wheels used for powering the northern mines when the River Alyn dried up in summer (water sank through swallow holes in the limestone river bed).

The path is well signposted and in frequent use by dog walkers. Continue past the remains of a 40 foot water wheel, formerly used to drain the early 19th century Glanalyn Lead Mine (17th Century to 1870). An adit on the right at the base of the cliffs was also used for drainage (the shafts were on top of the cliffs). Climb away from the river (*moving from Denbighshire into Flintshire*), past a house and kennels on the left, then go along the access drive to a metalled road. Cross this to continue as the Leete Path; the leete itself becomes much better defined as you pass mine entrances on the right and climb higher above the river.

Devil's Gorge at Loggerheads

Mine entrance off the Leete Path, Loggerheads

The Leete Path traversing high up the cliffs

Several waymarked paths diverge from the main path, but shortly go over a footbridge crossing Devil's Gorge, a near vertical cleft in the cliff popular with people abseiling. Paths descend to this so you can enter and examine the mine entrances, but return to the Leete Path which climbs higher above the river and locally closely skirts the vertical cliffs – though at the steepest bits there is a handrail.

Where the path meets a metalled road turn left, steeply downhill to the road bridge over the river; which all but disappears in summer, vanishing through the underlying limestone.

The next phase climbs up another limestone block, around a deep re-purposed quarry and through a wood rich in abandoned lead mine shafts, to descend through more woods on old lead mining terrain to Hendre in the deep Wheeler Valley.

From the bridge walk along the **Cilcain** road for a few metres then turn right on a waymarked bridleway to **Hesp Alyn** Farm just before a cottage. Go through the gate and head diagonally left across the narrow field with a hedge, caravan site and River Alyn beyond. Go through a steel gate, past a menage and modern stables on the right, and **Hesp Alyn** house on the left down to a track.

Hesp Alyn is a Grade II listed, probable late 17th Century two storey house with a 19th century extension.

Head left on the stony track, slightly uphill, and where the track bends left take the signed footpath right steeply uphill through a copse to a rickety wooden gate. Head half right on a grassy track between outbuildings and the white stone house of **Tan-y-rhiw**, slightly uphill with waymarkers pointing ahead into a wood. After a few metres there is a lean-to wood store with the back wall formed from the limestone cliff. The low cliff continues on the left of the track as the track ascends through the woods, to join a tarmac lane at its lowest point with a track down to Pandy Cottage (*"pandy" is a fulling mill*) to the right.

Turn right on the lane and at the top of the first steep section, at a little lay-by on the left, take the footpath left into the wood past a large quarried rock in the track. Follow the path as it steepens to a stile, going between more quarried rocks to reach a quarry track with derelict stone buildings opposite.

Turn right on the initially level track past a couple of brick buildings with large quarried blocks on the left The track climbs gradually through trees to reach a steel quarry gate at the top, where warnings of blasting are displayed.

*The **Trim Rock Quarry**, closed for some years, was restored in 2013 and is currently being monitored for habitat and species management.*

Turn right here onto a path into the predominantly beech wood of **Coed Du**, swinging round to the left around the quarry.

The wood contains many shafts resulting from 19th century lead mining. Though mainly level, at one point the path dips steeply down to the left across an old surface working with fenced off shafts to left and right.

At a well-endowed marker post (six arrows) go straight ahead past the ruins of a stone cottage. There are several paths in the wood, but keep heading slightly west of north and not downhill to the northeast.

On a much broader path there is a

The Afon Alun near Cilcain

waymarker post pointing half left via other waymarkers, down through a rocky bit to a stile, then ahead through new-growth deciduous woodland past another stile after 40 paces. On the back of a large tree on the left is a sign Yr Hafan and 10 metres further on, with the **Pen y Cefn Pasture SSSI** to your left, turn right along a path/bridleway and in 40 paces past a steel gate to a tarmac lane.

This SSSI is a 2.4 hectare (5.9 acre) site considered to be one of the best known surviving examples of a type of enclosed pasture on limestone. There are numerous uncommon plants including orchids (Green-winged, Fragrant and Common Spotted), Crosswort, Burnet Saxifrage, Betony and Burnet Rose.

Turn right on the lane, now with views to the eastern slopes of the Clwydian Range. Follow the lane past **Pen y Cefn**, *a 16th century two-storey Grade II listed minor gentry house*, to the second right hand bend, just past the house Fardo, where you take a signposted bridleway to the left. *This is the access track to* **Garreg Boeth** *and to Coed Cadw's (the Woodland Trust) Big Wood.*

In 50-60 paces turn right at a waymarker down the access drive to Carreg Boeth Cottage, taking a grassy track past the new house on the left behind gabions, and swing downhill to the right past a couple of abandoned buildings where the ground drops away on the left to reveal an old abandoned, overgrown quarry with woods to the right. The path skirts the quarry to a steel gate with waymarker.

This was an intensely mined area with old shafts shown on the map (and which may be visible today) probably from the 19th century Garreg Boeth lead mine.

Off to the right is an open clearing; go straight ahead, bearing right a few metres in front of an old abandoned cottage.

Follow the wood on the left at the edge of the field, then, on entering the wood, head downhill following the edge of the wood with grazing fields below on the left.

Go over the next stile to a tarmac lane, turn left downhill, with a large quarry in the valley ahead reaching up to the skyline. At the T junction, with the house **Coed Du** on the right, cross over heading downhill on a marked grassy footpath between high hedges. There is the sound of traffic on the main road, then houses can be seen along the valley bottom. Ignore the footpath off to the left, but continue down to the main road at **Hendre**.

Hendre today is a small, quiet village spread along the Wheeler Valley with the A541 running alongside the east-flowing river. In the past it was more heavily industrialised with steam trains running along the Mold-Denbigh Line (now abandoned). Lead mining and quarrying were important with the Olwyn Goch mine in the east of the village of particular importance. The shaft was deepened when the Milwr Tunnel reached Hendre, and was enlarged, later (1940's) being used to access underground limestone extraction by Pilkingtons for glass making. Underground chambers up to 80 ft. high remain, after extraction of 70,000-80,000 tons of limestone per annum. The Hendre Quarry, just north of the village, is still operational.

From Hendre climb through the ancient woodland of Coed y Felin, traversing fields and woods to the summit of Moel Ffagnallt overlooking the historic industrial landscape of Halkyn Mountain.

Cross the road to a footpath over a little bridge with Mill House on the left and Felin Newydd on the right. Go steeply uphill across a grassy patch to a wooden gate at the edge of the wood, Coed y Felin. Cross the course of the old railway line and head diagonally left uphill.

North Wales Wildlife Trust's **Coed y Felin** *is a 10 hectare (25 acre) site of ancient woodland on limestone with associated wild flowers and a nature trail. It contains oak, ash and planted sweet chestnut trees whilst the woodland floor and open meadows are rich in flowers through the seasons. Springtime is possibly best when the bluebells are out. There was much lead mining in the Hendre Valley and old mine shafts can still be seen in the woods.*

The path climbs, mostly gently, though

Path through the woods of Coed y Felin

with some steps, through the deciduous wood (with many sweet chestnut trees) until it meets a sunken path coming up from the left, which formerly connected Hendre to Cilcain Hall. Join this, swinging right and follow more steeply uphill until exiting the wood onto a stony track. Turn right, with views to the left over to Moel Famau. The track bends to the right where there is firstly a white cottage on the left then, behind high hedges, the sizeable building of **Cilcain Hall**.

Beyond the various outbuildings to the hall turn right at a surfaced lane (signs for Fron Far and Doggy Breaks Wales). Ignore the first footpath on the left, continuing past **Hersedd**, then take a signposted footpath left, over a wooden stile, into a field. *There is much evidence of past mining activity (old shafts and spoil heaps) which belonged to the Rhewl lead/silver mine of 1864–1877) or the Hersedd lead mine (1889–1893).* Pass a concrete water trough on the left, aiming for a steel gate and navigate, with difficulty, the stile on the left to a surface track where you turn right up to a little triangle of roads.

Turn left passing a house (**Rhewl**) on the left, then past Trellyniau Bach (mid 19th century) and shortly after **Trellyniau Fawr,** (an early 17th century two-storey stone house with slate roof) where you take the signed footpath off to the right down a stony track. Here, good views open up to the Clwydian Hills with the transmitter mast on **Moel y Parc** prominent. After a few metres the track bends to the right, but go left on a grassy path, which meanders through a narrow strip of open woodland or scrub with fields beyond.

Pass several small partially fenced overgrown quarries down to the left, before leaving the wood and going through gorse thickets. Here the view opens up to the northwest where a large active quarry is prominent. The path becomes muddier as farm buildings appear on the right, and goes over a stile with waymarker and through a small steel gate, then up a grassy path to the stony access drive to the **Moel Ffagnallt Farm.**

Turn right on the stony track for 200 metres when a grassy break through the gorse and bracken allows an ascent left to the open, rocky ground at the summit (287m, 942 ft. marked by a small concrete plug in the ground, though no trig point). *There are great views in all directions.*

For the next four kilometres you traverse the open access land of the former mining hotspot of Halkyn Mountain, climbing to its trig point for views to Snowdonia, Liverpool Bay and the Dee estuary, then continuing across the sheep-grazed Holywell Common via abandoned and well-shielded modern limestone quarries to the end of the stage in Brynford.

Head north, towards **Rhes-y-Cae** for a few metres to a millennium cairn built of dressed limestone, many of the blocks containing fossils of crinoids (sea lilies). To descend, head north towards the nearest house, on steep grass with bracken on the right.

Much of the high ground that you can see from here is part of the **Halkyn Mountain/Mynydd Helygain SAC** *(Special Area of Conservation), designated for its grasslands on soils rich in heavy metals, dry heaths, purple moor-grass meadows, dry grasslands and scrublands on limestone.*

The **Comin Helygain A GlaswellTiroedd Treffynnon/Halkyn Common and Holywell Grasslands SSSI** *comprises about 2.7 square miles of special interest for its minerals, flora and amphibian species including greater crested newts, notably in the abandoned quarry pools.*

Geologically the ancient mining landscape is important allowing study of the vein mineralisation of the Northeast Wales Orefield. The mineralisation occurs along east-west veins and north-south cross-courses with their positions picked out by lines of shafts and bell-pits sunk in search of lead ore. The mineralisation chiefly consists of galena (lead ore) and sphalerite (zinc ore) within calcite, fluorite and minor baryte. Uraninite-bearing hydrocarbons occur locally in the veins.

At the trig point on Halkyn Mountain

The soils of the SSSI are influenced by the underlying limestone, by glacial till and by spoil tips from mining; there is hence a wide variety of grasses, bryophytes and flowers.

Follow the stony track to the right round the left hand bend or take the grassy alternative as a shortcut. When the track bends to the right and another track comes in from the left, take the grassy path past the house on the left following the line of electricity poles heading towards Rhes y Cae.

Turn left on the metalled road at the Rhes y Cae village sign and after 15 paces fork right on a narrow grassy path which heads slightly uphill between gorse bushes to meet a stony track coming in from the left, goes between two sets of houses, and turns left at a metalled road just before another Rhes y Cae village sign. In a few metres there are fenced off mine shafts on the left and houses to the right.

Turn right at the crossroads and head north, uphill, on the road out of the village. This part of Halkyn Mountain is criss-crossed by paths and it may be difficult to select the right one to arrive at the trig point. Fork right on a path after 75m then left off this main path in 100m. Fenced off

Looking north from Moel Ffagnallt to Halkyn Mountain and the active limestone quarry of Pant-y-pwll-dŵr

shafts and limestone outcrops, possibly representing old linear open workings, are evident. The path climbs, initially parallel to the road off to the left, then veers right, until at a major cross-path it turns left and heads steeply up to the trig point of **Halkyn Mountain** (283m, 928 ft.; not shown on OS map).

Views are extensive, both inland and down to the Dee Estuary, Wirral and Liverpool.

From here take any path heading northwest to cross one road, then down another path to join a busier road.

The North Wales Limestone Way

Follow the road downhill left, then, opposite a path into **Pant-y-pwll-dŵr Quarry** on the left fork right up the Aberdo Quarry road for 100m, taking care to avoid quarry lorries, passing under two sets of power lines and steadily climbing.

At Pant-y-pwll-dŵr Quarry, blasting takes place about once a week with each blast loosening about 20,000 tonnes of rock, sufficient to lay one mile of single-carriageway asphalt road. The siren sounds before and during blasting; it can be heard from Moel Ffagnallt, although little can be seen due to the quarry screening and the depth of the current quarry hole. About 800,000 tonnes of limestone are quarried here each year.

The Aberdo Quarry is named after the type of limestone quarried, formerly known as Aberdo Limestone. It consists of interbedded clay-bearing limestones and mudstones, the mixture of which is used to produce hydraulic lime, suitable for underwater construction as in docks and bridges.

Up to the right are the workings of the now-abandoned **Pen yr Henblas** Quarry.

Just a few paces past the second set of power lines, there is a concrete marker in the verge.

This indicates the route of the 24 inch gas

Marker for the 24 inch gas pipeline that delivers gas from offshore fields to Connah's Quay power station

pipeline that takes gas from the Liverpool Bay offshore fields to the power station at Connah's Quay.

As the quarry road starts descending, fork left to follow the wide green path over rough ground between capped shafts to a track and houses. Turn right up the track, passing four large agricultural sheds on the left, and head uphill towards the Grade II listed **Waen y Brodlas** limekiln complex.

*The block of five large kilns at **Waen-y-Brodlas** were designed for high output of lime. Hydraulic lime from here was used to build*

The industrial limekilns of Waen-y-Brodlas

docks at Liverpool, Birkenhead and Belfast between 1860 and 1890, but lime burning on Halkyn ended around 1914. The kilns were restored to their present state over the summer of 2013; the biggest job was for Kiln 2 where 25 to 30 tonnes of material had to be dug out by hand. An information board gives details.

Follow the stony track below the kilns heading northwest along Pant y Pydew and along the eastern edge of Holywell Common, ignoring the fork off to the left. Swing left in front of an old quarry face; through grassland, gorse and hawthorn bushes/trees, finally going downhill to reach a metalled road with the Crooked Horn Inn ahead at the end of the stage.

The nearest accommodation is at the Glan yr Afon Inn which is just over a kilometre away. To reach it follow the rough road northeast with the Crooked Horn Inn on your left, down to a footbridge over the A55. Carry on downhill until meeting a surfaced road (the Milwr-Dolphin road). Turn right and in 200 metres, where the road bends right, fork left to the inn. Holywell accommodation, about 2km away, would be possible via taxi.

Stage 7: Brynford to Prestatyn

Start:	Brynford, The Crooked Horn Inn (SJ 18657 74073)
Finish:	Prestatyn Hillside Car Park (SJ 07162 82113)
Distance:	20.2km (12.6 miles)
Ascent:	410m (1345 feet)
Time:	5 hours 13 minutes

Stage Summary: Starting with a traverse of an open common proceeding by field paths with estuary views to a friary then field and woodland paths to an old Celtic Cross, field paths and villages to a magnificent hilltop ancient monument and a descent through fields and old villages finishing along the clifftop path of Offa's Dyke Path and down flights of steps to finish at the base of the cliffs and the end of the walk. *Continue down through streets of the seaside resort of Prestatyn to the bus and train stations.*

Refreshment: St. Pio's Café, Pantasaph is a café/restaurant open daily except Mondays. The Druid Inn, Gorsedd (pub and restaurant) (01352 713975) is just off the route.

Note that the "Rock at Lloc" is now closed. The Crown Inn, Trelawnyd serves meals and drinks and is said to be always open. *The Eagle and Child Inn, Gwaenysgor is a pub and restaurant. There are numerous establishments in Prestatyn.*

Transport: Prestatyn is on the London to Holyhead mainline route. It is also well connected by buses running along the coast to Rhyl, Colwyn Bay and Llandudno to the west and to Holywell, Flint and Chester to the east. There are inland services to St. Asaph, Denbigh and beyond. Service 19 (Rhyl, Prestatyn, Flint) goes through Trelawnyd, Berthengam, Whitford, Gorsedd and Carmel on an approximate two-hour service. Service 14C (Mold-Holywell) goes through Brynford, Gorsedd, Pantasaph; other rural bus services run infrequently.

Accommodation: Celyn Villa B&B is 1km north of the route at Carmel; Morgan's B&B, Axton is on the route; Pantasaph Farm B&B is 150m south of the route (shown on the OS map); Numerous in Prestatyn.

As a Day Trip: Bus services are scarce in Brynford, although parking is easy opposite

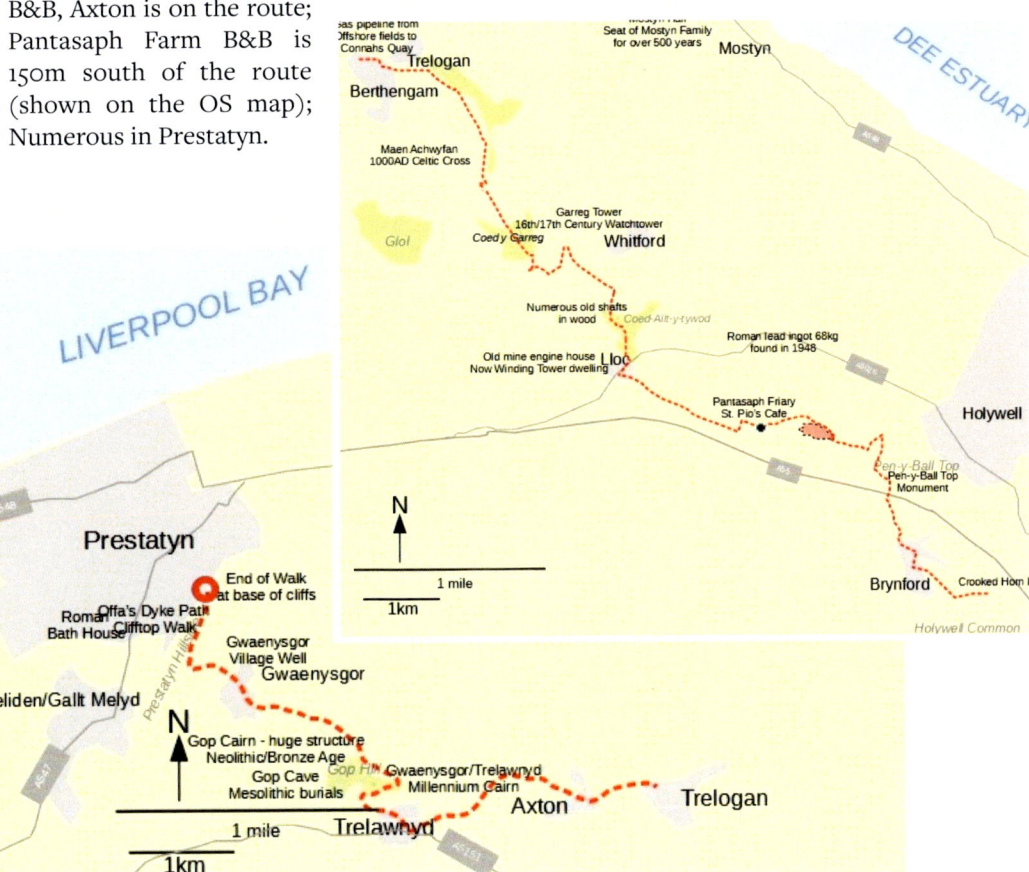

The North Wales Limestone Way 109

The Sustrans marker on Holywell Common, opposite the Crooked Horn Inn

Halkyn Mountain information board, Brynford

the Crooked Horn Inn. With two cars one car could be parked at the small Hillside car park at the end of the stage and the second taken to Brynford. Alternatively, with a single car, take a taxi from the Hillside car park to Brynford.

The walk

Start by continuing across Holywell Common to Pen y Ball Top with its views down to Liverpool and the Dee Estuary. Traverse pasture to a Franciscan Friary, then through fields and post-industrial woods to Coed y Garreg and its 17th century watchtower.

From the Crooked Horn Inn, cross the road to the Sustrans "totem pole" next to a Halkyn Mountain information board on a large rock and take the wide stony track heading west across the common.

Ignore side paths, but as the path descends giving great views to the Snowdonia peaks, in 200m turn right under power lines. The main path continues off to the left in a more northwesterly direction. Pass a fenced off shaft on the left then keep the white cottage (Meifod) close to the left (the narrow path forking to the right here leads

Sheep wander freely in Brynford

Sculpted figures on Brynford village green representing generations of men and boys who worked in the lead mines and quarries

to an old quarry) and bear right on the wide stony access track, swinging left at the T junction on a grassy track through gorse bushes and hawthorn trees. Aim for the white-painted "blockhouse" next to the football pitch, with the church ahead and houses to the left to take a track between houses to reach the metalled road (the B5121). On the left is a shop (with post office) and on the right the old schoolhouse. Turn right on the road for 100m, past St. Michael's Church to **Brynford** crossroads. *The church was built 1851–53 in early Gothic-revival style to replace the promised church at Pantasaph, when its founders, Lord and Lady Feilding, converted to Roman Catholicism.*

Turn left, passing the village green *with sculpted figures representing the generations of men and boys who worked in the mines and quarries*, and just past the last houses on the right, fork right down a stony track along the edge of the **Holywell Golf Club** course with scattered houses on the right. Turn right on the bridge over the A55 expressway noting the Pen-y-Ball monument visible on the little hill ahead, with the track forking left in 100m.

To examine the Pen y Ball Monument (Mon on the OS map), in 20m by an electricity

The North Wales Limestone Way

pole, take the winding path heading uphill through scrub and gorse. This prominent Halkyn-stone monolith erected to commemorate the marriage of the Duke of York, heir to the English Throne, in 1893. It is on a circular mound with stone steps leading up to the obelisk. It is worth visiting for the all-round views.

Take the stony track to a "T" junction with Sunnyside facing. Turn left and in 30m by a fenced-off shaft on the bank on the left (lead and silver mining was intense around here from the early 18th century), fork right on a narrow path across scrub and rough hummocky grass towards an electricity pole next to a stile with path beyond through a field. Go uphill, through a wide gap between trees, and alongside the hawthorns and wall on the right to cross a wooden stile.

Just before the stile, note several round depressions in the scrub to the right. These are believed to be medieval "boles" (hence Pen-y-Ball) the depressions being where lead was smelted close to where the ore was mined. The boles were situated on high ground exposed to strong winds.

Continue ahead to the trig point (**Pen y Ball Top** 255m, 837 ft.) from where there

The Dee Estuary from Pen y Ball Top trig point

are views down to **Holywell**, the Dee Estuary, **Mostyn Quay** (now the Port of Mostyn), the North Wales coast and inland to the Clwydian Hills and Snowdonia, then continue in the same line downhill to the nearer of two stiles in the fence on the left, next to an electricity pole.

Mostyn Quay *has figured several times in British history; Henry Bolingbroke disembarked at Mostyn Quay on his way to Flint Castle to wrest the crown from Richard II (see Stage 2).*

Once over the stile, turn back sharp left to follow the line of wooden electricity poles uphill to a stile in the field corner. Go along the field edge to the next stile and an old fenced quarry on the right (known locally as Black Limestone).

*Down on the left is a cutting, with a tunnel linking the quarries on the south side of the ridge through to the old quarry on the north. A tramway was built by Holywell Lime Company in 1848 linking these quarries and others down to **Greenfield Dock** at Holywell. The Black Limestone quarried was a mixture of limestone with some clay and was the ideal mixture for preparing hydraulic lime (lime that set underwater) that was used in docks (including Liverpool, Birkenhead and Belfast) and bridges (Menai and Runcorn).*

Follow the fence on the right, with the tunnel and tramway beneath your feet, until the most-worn path bears left diagonally towards the top side of gorse thickets; take the path as it winds through the gorse to return to the fence. By a large sycamore tree next to the fence bear diagonally left down the field to the corner of the house garden (by a wood store) and, keeping to the left of the house, cross stiles here either side of the access track, then turn up right behind the house.

Turn half-left to go around the edge of

The Franciscan Friary at Pantasaph

the fenced off White Limestone Quarry (a pure limestone used to build the nearby church, friary, convent and school; it closed in 1912). The path leaves the quarry fence and heads half right to a waymarked (Pilgrims Way) path junction and stile at a small copse. There is no obvious path across the field and there has been much agricultural improvement (removal of fences/hedges) recently. The east – west field boundary no longer exists and much scrub has been cleared. The best route is to head in a direct line, via a double electricity pole (with waymarkers pointing half left) for the top edge of the wood ahead (west)

The North Wales Limestone Way

where a shiny steel gate can shortly be seen.

As you come closer you can see the wall that defines the edge of the wood. Head alongside this down to the left, gently at first, then more steeply with buildings appearing ahead, until you reach the bottom right corner of the field at a wall junction. Go through the elongated kissing gate with a house on the right. Head downhill, slightly left, on a stony track which shortly meets a metalled lane. To the right is a steel barrier and straight ahead a stone slab stile with metal handrail in a wall. Go over this into the churchyard of the **Pantasaph Franciscan Friary** with a waymarker for Pilgrims Way, the church immediately on the right and graveyard on the left.

The path becomes surfaced and passes through a wrought iron gate into the car park.

A little signpost points to various facilities including toilets and tearoom (St. Pio's Café).

In 1849 the Bishop of St. Asaph laid the foundation stone for the building of a new church at Pantasaph and building work began, but the following year the sponsors, the Feildings, converted to Catholicism and decided the church was to be for Catholic worship. New Anglican churches were built at Gorsedd and Brynford. Franciscan friars arrived at Pantasaph and the friary (with the Stations of the Cross – designed by Pugin) became the UK centre for the Capuchins. A Pilgrims' house and guesthouse were completed for the numerous pilgrims that travelled here and in time St. Clare's Convent and Orphanage and two schools were built on the other side of Monastery Road. The schools and convent shut many years ago and have been converted into housing, but the church and friary still attract Catholic worshippers. The Retreat Centre closed in 2017, but day visitors are still welcome.

The route continues along the top of the car park then a path with hedges on each side, to reach a metalled road. Turn left (waymarker) along the row of Scots Pines down to Monastery Road at a T junction. On the opposite side of the road are buildings originally associated with the friary, now converted to housing.

Turn right along the pavement (shortly changing to a grass verge) past an old-style red telephone box (not working) – with noise from the A55 on the left – to a further T junction. Turn right for 10 metres and

Former engine house for Merllyn West lead mine

Bluebells in Coed Allt-y-tywod

cross the road at the village sign for **Gorsedd**. Cross the waymarked stile and take the footpath (signed **Lloc** ½ and Pant y Wacco ½) along the hedge at the right edge of the field. In the far-right field corner cross the waymarked wooden stile into a small wood, downhill to a grassy area then bear right to meet a track. Turn left and in 20 metres join a metalled road with the village signs for **Pant y Wacco** on the left and for Gorsedd on the right. *The OS map shows this as a Roman Road, and it is believed to lie on the course of the Chester – Caernarfon road.*

Head straight across the road and down the road opposite (No Entry sign) and in 100 paces turn right at the main Holywell road and cross to the far pavement. *The pub that was on the corner, The Rock at Lloc, has now closed, and is awaiting conversion to a private dwelling.*

On the left, over the beech hedge of the house "Winding Tower", can be seen a house conversion of a late eighteenth to 19th century two-storey pumping engine house. The next house, "Ty Maen" has a carved stone at the left gatepost "1777" and on the right "230 yards above sea level", presumably linking to the

The North Wales Limestone Way

days of lead mining. The engine house was used for pumping water from the Merllyn West mine which accessed the western end of the Merllyn east-west lead/silver vein. This lies just north of the rich Holloway Vein which runs under Lloc, Gorsedd and Carmel and was mined on a large scale since 1773 by the Holywell Level Company (owned by Sir Pyers Mostyn and Thomas Pennant). It had high proportions of silver and calamine (secondary zinc ore) with the lead. Numerous shafts are shown on OS maps and remains are still visible in the wood to the east. The Romans were probably the first to mine for lead in the area, sinking shafts around **Carmel** *2km to the east. In 1948, when digging the foundations for Carmel School, a Roman lead ingot weighing 150 pounds was uncovered.*

Take the second footpath to the left, just before a house at the corner of **Coed Allt-y-tywod**. In 10 metres go right round a full-width wooden gate and head straight, ignoring the fork to the right. In a few metres bear right on the main path and soon pass to the left around a garage-sized wooden building.

Continue on the wide path (numerous bluebells in spring), heading gently downhill with evidence of mining activity (shafts and spoil heaps), turning left at a marked path junction and continuing to the edge of the wood where the right hand waymarked wooden stile gives access to a large sloping field.

Over to the left is the wooded hill, **Coed y Garreg**. Go alongside the hedge on the left down the field edge to the field corner and turn left onto a farm track which in 10 metres joins a public bridleway at a steel gate. Go straight ahead (blue marker arrow) along the sunken bridleway, with old hedges on both sides.

A track from **Hollow Farm** joins from the left, but continue straight ahead for

Sunken bridleway near Hollow Farm

The watchtower in Coed y Garreg

0.5km to a metalled road. Cross the road to follow the bridleway (*a direct, though less scenic, footpath to the farmyard goes left over a stile and across the field*) through a kissing gate eventually curving round left, through the leftmost kissing gate at the apex of the bend, to follow the base of the rocky slope and reach, through a further wooden gate, the farmyard at **Garreg Farm**.

Cross the farmyard, passing between the farmhouse and outbuildings, through a steel gate and along the bridleway beyond. After the next gate the way turns half right then up the right edge of the field up a partly wooded section through another gate and up a slope to a concrete farm track with the Mannod Appaloosa Stud Farm to the right. Turn left along the access track and at the top of the rise turn sharp right just past a letter box up the access track towards a cottage (Garreg Uchaf). With the cottage to the right fork left up a grassy path, with fence and tumbledown wall on the left, to go into **Coed y Garreg**. In 10 metres turn left uphill on the Pilgrims Way along a forest ride, which is followed until the edge of the wood where a stile gives access to the field beyond. Just before this stile, one path heads downhill to the left and another uphill to the right.

It is worthwhile taking the short detour right on this uphill path as it leads to the **Tower**. *From here there are good views of the Dee and Mersey estuaries and beyond, depending on the state of the surrounding trees. In any case there is a useful tree trunk seat. The watchtower itself is locked and barred. The tower is circular, about 6.5m in diameter, and tapers in stages. There is an iron-gated entrance, although no floors survive. It is probably 16th to 17th century (rather than the Roman Pharos suggested, amongst others, by Thomas Pennant writing in 1796). It is broadly similar to the towers at*

The 1000AD Maen Achwyfan Cross

Bryniau (Stage 1) and above Abergele (Stage 2) used to warn of sea raiders. It was restored for the diamond jubilee of 1897.

Descend Coed y Garreg, calling in to see the 1000 year old Celtic cross of Maen Achwyfan. Traverse fields to the Domesday village of Trelawnyd, then climb the superb viewpoint of Gop Hill to examine Gop Cairn, Wales' largest prehistoric monument.

Return to the stile at the wood edge with views ahead to the coast and offshore wind farms and to the left, **Gop Hill**. Cross the large field diagonally downhill in the direction of the waymarkers, aiming for the far right corner via an intermediate fence and stile. When you are part way down the field you can aim for the cottage and walled garden in the corner and climb the stone-step stile in the wall to reach the road beyond. Turn left then, in a few metres, right at the junction. The route takes the next road right, but first it is worth taking the main road left for a few metres to visit **Maen Achwyfan** in the field on the left, accessed via a kissing gate and short path.

The Maen Achwyfan Cross is a particularly fine, richly carved, 3.4m high, slightly tapering monolithic slab-cross with a circular head; the tallest wheelcross in Britain. It has been dated to 1000AD and is believed to belong to a Northumbrian tradition, heavily influenced by Viking design. The name Maen Achwyfan is thought to be derived from "Stone of Cwyfan"; in the 7th century there was a Saint Cwyfan and there is today a St Cwyfan's church in Llangwyfan 13km south at the foot of the Clwydian Range.

Return to the road and take the minor road signposted **Whitford**/Chwitffordd. In 20 paces turn left down a marked bridleway. There is a cottage on the left and on the right a narrow strip of immature woodland. Go through a steel gate and shortly double gates either side with on the right a sign indicating "Mostyn Estates Private Woodland" and the start of a mature wood that continues on the right of the bridleway. The bridleway is a fine, wide, slightly gravelly vehicle track. It swings round to the left and just before the bend sharpens, with a white wooden gate ahead, fork right along the path "Pennant Walk and North Wales Pilgrims Way".

In a few metres, where a steel gate leads into a field with a farm beyond, turn right on a more grassy bridleway down the edge of the wood. At the end of the bridleway is a steel gate with a wooden stile and a sign saying "Mostyn Estates Ltd, Public Footpath Only". There are waymarkers for the Pilgrims Way, left here and in a few metres another steel gate, but no stile. Go through the gate along a grassy path enclosed by hedges each side to another gate ahead.

At the wooden gateway there is an electric fence across the field and waymarkers for the Pilgrims Way and Flintshire County Council pointing slightly right across the field. Unclip the electric fence and go through, closing it behind you, and aim to the left of the tall trees in the hedge almost directly ahead. The two trees are halfway between the stile and the edge of the wood. Cross the stile and angle half right down to the wood edge and follow this to the field corner where there is a prominent wooden fence and stile.

Head over the waymarked stile and bend round to the left with bracken and gorse to the right and an open field to the left. The path now goes along the edge of the wood where there is another Mostyn Estates Public Footpath sign and a path snaking off into the wood. Go straight

Steeply dipping beds of Pentre Chert in Trelogan Quarry

ahead through a kissing gate and gate with a waymarker for the Pilgrims Way pointing half left heading along a field boundary with the wood receding to the right. In the corner of the field go through a kissing gate with rough ground to the right and field to the left. This rough ground is part of the **Glaswelltdiroedd Trelogan/Trelogan Grasslands SSSI**.

This 10.84 hectare (27 acre) site, split across several areas to the northeast of Trelogan, is of special interest for its open vegetation on soils rich in heavy metals. The underlying geology is the Carboniferous Pentre Chert Formation, but the whole area is dissected by faults and the site contains spoil derived from lead and zinc mining. Much of the site is ungrazed by domestic livestock and parts of the site have been extensively studied by researchers from Liverpool University looking at metal-tolerant species to assist with reclamation of difficult substrates.

Fork right on a well-used path across the rough ground, winding between rough grass, brambles and gorse, via an open area with a quarry below on the right, to reach a stony vehicle track. Bear right and take the track downhill to reach a road.

Those interested in geology can turn right for a few paces to look at the abandoned quarry (now with a few industrial units). The quarry contains steeply dipping thin-bedded strata of the Pentre Chert Formation, which overlies the Carboniferous Limestone and represents deeper water (slope) deposition. It is found only in this region of Northeast Wales (Trelogan-Halkyn). It is said that this cherty (or flinty) rock gives its name to the county (Flintshire).

About a further 1km northeast of the quarry was the Trelogan Mine (lead, silver, zinc), which operated from about 1700 to the early 1900s. Much of the rough ground around Trelogan is the site of old mine workings, spoil

Marker for gas pipeline near Trelogan

tips or processing areas. Individual shafts can still be recognised in the fields as small, circular, uncultivated areas.

The route itself turns left and heads to a crossroads with the Afon Goch public house on the left. This is being converted to a house though (in 2019) the pub signs were still up. Go straight across at the crossroads and uphill along the lane. A few metres before the next crossroads there are marker signs each side of the road for a gas pipeline; *these indicate the route of the 24 inch gas pipeline that takes gas from the Liverpool Bay fields to the power station at Connah's Quay.*

Continue up the road, then 20m past a house on the left take a signposted (footpath sign on a pole) gravelly track uphill to the right towards the scattered hillside houses of **Axton**.

Where the track bends more sharply to the right, on the apex of the bend, go left over a waymarked stile on a somewhat sunken path enclosed by hedges. Bend round to the right, slightly uphill, over another stile to reach a small field with a half-wall coming towards you. Go left round the wall and through a kissing gate to reach a stony track with farm buildings and houses off to the right. Turn left through an open gateway or hidden kissing gate. Head uphill with houses ahead, through double steel gates and a green kissing gate to a tarmac lane with "Hillside" house down to the left and, on the right, Bryn Redyn.

Turn right up the road and almost at the top of the hill there is an impressive dressed sandstone gateway with wrought iron gates, entryphone system and security cameras. To the right of the gate there is a footpath sign and stile. It is worthwhile here just going over the stile and along the grassy path for a few tens of metres, past the Welsh Water Axton covered reservoir on top of the hill just to see the views over the estuary.

Return to and cross the road to go over a slightly overgrown stile to a footpath flanked by hedges. There is an intermediate hedge and stile, not shown on the OS map, with a fine hedge on the right. Standing on top of the stile, looking over the hedge you can see two humps in the field; these are Bronze Age funeral barrows.

From the next stile at the field corner head along by the hedge aiming towards the cottage off to the right. To the left the

Stone slab stile typical of the area, Trelawnyd

ground is hummocky with shafts and spoil tips – looks like a First World War battleground. Across the field the cottage has a sign "Morgan's B&B, morgansbedandbreakfast.co.uk". Go alongside the field boundary to an open gateway (or over the stile) to reach a bridleway with waymarkers pointing left and right.

Turn left along the slightly stony bridleway. After about 20 paces at a large limestone rock near the hedge on the right, fork right on a path heading for a wooden stile ahead. The path crosses a very hummocky field aiming for the forested top of **Gop Hill** ahead. Climb to a cairn on the near skyline, the Gwaenysgor-Trelawnyd Millennium Cairn, capped by a circular panorama, inscribed with the old names of the villages going back to Doomsday Time. There are great views all round including Snowdonia and the Clwydian Range.

Head left to a field corner through a kissing gate, past an aerial and round to the left near the top of the hill at 230m (755 ft.) is a seat with the Welsh flag colours red, white and green stripes on the backrest. The path heads down the ridge past a marker post then swings left towards a stile in the bottom right field corner. There are two wooden stiles here as the twin fences protect a juvenile hedge, though badger activity is still evident. Keep the wall, hedge and fence to your right then turn left along the bottom of the field with mature trees in the hedge on the right and outcropping limestone to the left. At an electricity pole ahead go over a stone slab stile and follow the line of poles across the field towards a white house on the road.

Go over the stile at the bottom of the field and down five or six stone steps to the road. Turn right, then just past the house turn left at a footpath pole/sign, over a stone slab stile with faded waymarkers on a post. The grassy path goes along the hedge on the left and becomes boggy as it nears a fenced-off muddy pond by a solitary big tree. Turn left over a stile (missing waymarkers) into the next field with another muddy pond on the left. Turn right, roughly along the hedge, through the muddy field (ponies) and a cross-hedge, to go over a wooden slab stile in the right hand corner with the fenced back gardens of houses of **Trelawnyd** to the left. The path goes straight ahead over a stone slab stile then left on a surfaced path, over a second stone slab stile, and along a gravelly drive to reach a tarmac road. Head right then left towards a chapel on Chapel Street, along the street to reach High Street.

Gwaenysgor and *Trelawnyd* *share a community council. Both are ancient villages recorded in the Domesday Book and both contain buildings still in use which date back to the 17th Century.*

A settlement, Rivelenoit, was recorded in the Domesday Book (which covered England, although at the time parts of North East Wales were part of Mercia) on this site, but the first

The scheduled ancient monument of Gop Cairn atop Gop Hill

Orchids on the slopes of Gop Hill, Trelawnyd

The North Wales Limestone Way

recorded occurrence of the name Trelawnyd was in the 17th century. A local industrial pioneer, John Wynne (1650–1714) living at what is now Gop Farm, coined the name "Newmarket" as he set about developing the village, with the aim of attracting custom and developing into a market town. This name is used on the 1st Edition Ordnance Survey map of the area. In 1954 the name was changed to Trelawnyd. The village is still based on farming, with most of the land owned by the Mostyn and Golden Grove Estates.

The Trelawnyd Male Voice Choir, formed in 1933 (when the village was Newmarket) is today one of the most accomplished and largest choirs in North Wales; it still rehearses in the Village Hall.

Turn right, uphill, on the road past the village car park to turn left along the drive after Bron Haul (footpath sign) and continue either through a gate across grass in front of a house and through a tall wooden gate or go left on a permissive path round the fenced garden. Both ways reach a stone-slab stile which is crossed to the open hillside of **Gop Hill**.

Much of the south-facing hillside here is part of the Moel Hiraddug and Bryn Gop SSSI.

Bryn Gop is a 12.7 hectare (31.4 acre) site

The entrance to Gop Cave on the slopes of Gop Hill

which includes Gop Cairn and the steep south-facing limestone grassland slopes above Trelawnyd. It is dominated by sheep – and horse-grazed grassland with patches of gorse, blackthorn and hawthorn. The site is noted for hoary rock-rose, spring cinquefoil and large populations of green-winged orchid and autumn lady's-tresses.

Take the footpath through the grassy field, avoiding gorse bushes, to a signpost. Turn right steeply uphill between gorse bushes and head slightly left. To visit **Gop Cave** aim further left; for the **Cairn** go directly uphill to cross a wall at the corner of the forest.

Here there is a wooden bench with **Gop Cairn** directly ahead; coniferous forest wraps round the cairn on three sides, though recently the trees have been cut back and the cairn is much better displayed. There are impressive views in all directions from the summit.

Gop Cave is an overhanging rock shelter with caves leading off. It was explored from the late 19th century and yielded many burials, prehistoric flints and pottery dating from the Mesolithic.

Gop Cairn, a Scheduled Monument and Wales' largest prehistoric monument, is a huge cairn, 75-80m in diameter and 12m high visible from much of the surrounding area. It was explored in the late 19th century by a shaft sunk to its centre, but this shed little light on its original purpose and it remains an enigma to this day. Modern opinion is that it is of Neolithic to Bronze Age origin.

Traverse the wooded Gop Hill to reach the old village of Gwaenysgor, then through fields to the edge of the limestone plateau. Join the Offa's Dyke Path for an airy walk on the steep hillside above Prestatyn, then descend across the slope to the base of the limestone crags and end of the walk. The well-preserved remains of a Roman bathhouse are a 1.5km walk, or taxi ride, away.

From the cairn head east on the permissive path that skirts the wood then enters it on the left and meanders through, passing several small quarries (presumably where the limestone blocks that were used in cairn-building came from) to reach a gate and wall stile at the corner of the wood.

Turn left down the field then in 80 paces go through a kissing gate into a field below the wood. In a further 35 paces re-enter the wood at a kissing gate. Just before entering the wood look to the north where on the hillside opposite there is a fine mansion, **Golden Grove**.

Golden Grove is a Grade I listed 16th Century mansion with landscaped gardens set in extensive grounds running to 1000 acres. The site on which it stands was first mentioned in the Domesday Book. It was built by Sir Edward Morgan – an official at the court of Elizabeth I – in 1578 and stayed in the family for 200 years, until it was sold in 1877. Today it is luxury bed and breakfast accommodation.

Turn right then head uphill and shortly turn right down a wide path carpeted with beech leaves downhill, until leaving the wood just above the rear of **Carn ychain** Farm, and along the bottom of the wood to a kissing gate. Turn right on a permissive path between farm buildings to the concreted farmyard.

Take the farm drive to a lane, turn left and ascend a bank to a kissing gate and into a field. Head diagonally across the first field aiming for an isolated tree then along the hedge-line to a kissing gate into the next field. Continue in the same line to a kissing gate into the third field. Here notice the round Bronze Age barrow (**Tumulus**) some 15m in diameter just after entering the field. Then cut off the corner of this field, bearing half right to reach the stile onto the farm track next to an electricity pole. Follow the track to a metalled road and turn right uphill past the 17th century farms Tŷ Isaf and Tŷ Uchaf into **Gwaenysgor**.

Gwaenysgor is also an ancient village recorded in the Domesday Book and contains buildings still in use which date back to the 17th Century and beyond.

St Mary's Church *on Ffordd Llyn Goch appears in the Domesday Book (described as "wasted)", and is believed to have had a Saxon foundation, although the circular shape of the graveyard suggests that it may have been a Romano-British cemetery. The church was probably rebuilt in Norman times, after 1100AD. It has many interesting historic features. Parish registers, implemented in the days of Henry VIII, still exist dating from 1538.*

The Eagle and Child Inn was originally a stone-built farmhouse, converted to an inn more than 100 years ago; it is also a restaurant.

Continue up the main street and turn left down Ffordd y Ffynnon on the Clwydian Way which shortly turns into a grassy path leading to the old village well at a crossroads of paths. *This was the source of water for the village until 1932 when standpipes were introduced, although mains water wasn't supplied to all homes until after the Second World War.*

Continue directly ahead before swinging left below minor crags and around a small rise (211m, 692 ft.) on which is a Bronze Age burial mound. The path meets a stile at a T junction with the Offa's Dyke Path, where you turn right, gaining superb views over the coastal plain towns of **Rhyl** and **Prestatyn** to the Great Orme and, on a clear day, the peaks of Snowdonia. *The path now represents the*

The old village well at Gwaenysgor

The final stages of the walk on Prestatyn Hillside

boundary between Denbighshire, below on the left, and Flintshire, on the right.

The hillside below is the **Prestatyn Hillside SSSI**. *The 24.5 hectare (60 acre) Prestatyn Hillside has been cited for three principal botanical features; semi-natural broadleaved woodland where sessile oak, ash, wild cherry, wych elm, rowan, hazel and dogwood predominate. Calcareous grassland with sheep's fescue, oat-grasses and quaking grass, and rare plants including hoary rock-rose, spring cinquefoil and a broad-leaved Helleborine. Bird's nest orchid and Greater butterfly orchid have been recorded.*

The path continues along the top of steep slopes, thankfully with a fence separating off the steep quarry faces below, down several flights of steps and through woodland with sessile oak and ash, to end at a small car park at the base of the limestone cliffs and the end of the walk.

To reach bus and train stations continue on the well-marked Offa's Dyke Path through the town's residential and shopping streets.

Prestatyn *may be best known as a Victorian seaside resort, but it has a long history dating back to pre-Roman times (an Iron Age hillfort at Moel Hiraddug 4km to the south is the northernmost of the Clwydian*

The remains of the Roman bath house, Prestatyn, a short way from the end of the walk

Range hillforts) A Roman bath house was re-excavated in Prestatyn in 1984 and it is believed that the Romans came to the area for the lead deposits near Meliden. Silver and possibly lead were mined through the Middle Ages, and from the mid 18th century zinc and lead became more profitable, reaching a peak in the mid 19th century. The mine closed in 1884. Prestatyn developed as a resort when the North Wales Coast line (Chester to Holyhead) arrived in 1848.

The preserved remains of the **Roman bath house** (SJ 06215 81752) are on Melyd Avenue, just a 1.5km walk from the end of the North Wales Limestone Way. Although it is within a housing development and occupies little more than a standard building plot, it is a quiet site with trees providing shade to one side and benches to sit on and contemplate.

The bath house, now a Scheduled Ancient Monument, was discovered in the 1930s and re-excavated in 1984. It was a masonry-built three-room building with changing room, warm room, hot room and cold plunge bath. Remains of the supports of a timber aqueduct supplying water to the baths have also been discovered. One of the tiles discovered at the site was made at the works of the 20th legion at Holt, near Chester, some 40 miles away. It is unusual in that it contains an imprint of a dog's paw, presumably acquired as the tiles were left out to dry in the sun. The site is also known for a number of clay moulds for bronze brooches, suggesting that bronze smiths were working locally. It is now thought that the site was civilian/industrial, with no presence of a Roman auxiliary fort.

Appendix 1: Glossary of Welsh Place Names

Translations from Welsh place names and other features are given below in the order in which they are encountered on the stages. There is always some uncertainty as to the correct meaning, and it is worth consulting a more authoritative source (see Further Reading).

Stage 1
Llandudno (church of St. Tudno)
Pen-y-Gogarth (Great Orme)
Mynydd Isaf (lower mountain)
Penrhynside (side of the promontory)
Mynydd Pant (mountain of the hollow)
Hen Dŵr (old water)
Bryn Euryn (Euryn's hill)
Nant y Gamar (Gamar stream)
Penmaen-bach (small headland of stone)
Coed Gelli (wood of the grove)
Bryn Maelgwyn (hill of Maelgwyn – the prince of the hounds)
Ty'n-y-Coed (house in the wood)
Bodysgallen Hall (house among thistles or the abode of Cadwallon)
Llandrillo-yn-rhos (church of St Trillo on the moor)
Llys Euryn (Euryn's court or hall)

Stage 2
Penmaenhead (stone headland)
Llysfaen (stone court or hall)
Tŷ Mawr (big house)
Mynydd Marian (gravelly mountain)
Craig y Forwyn (Maiden's Leap)
Afon Dulas (River Dulas)
Rhyd y Foel (ford of the bare hill)
Garth Gogof (promontory, hill or enclosure of the cave)
Coed Gopa (wooded crest or summit)
Castell Cawr (Giant's Castle)
Tan-y-Gopa (under or beneath the summit)

Stage 3
Afon Gele (Gele River)
Moelfre Isaf (lower bald hill
Coed Pen-y-Bryn (wood at the top of the hill)
Mynydd y Gaer (fort of the mountain)
Nant-Luke (Luke's stream)
Nant Bach (little stream)
Bryn Hen (old hill)
Plas Newydd (new mansion)
Ysgubor Newydd (new barn)
Cefn Meiriadog (Meiriadog's ridge)

The North Wales Limestone Way

Bont Newydd (new bridge)
Coed y Dafarn (wood of the tavern)
Henllan (old church)
Denbigh (from the Welsh Dinbych, little fort)

Stage 4
Pont Ystrad (bridge of the valley or river meadow)
Nant Mawr (big stream, dingle or glen)
Pentre Llanrheadr (homestead or village of the church of the waterfall)
Afon Clywedog (audible river)
Coed Duon (black or dark wood)
Nant Goch (red stream or glen)
Ty'n-y-caeau (small farm of the enclosure)
Ruthin (red fort)
Llanfair Dyffryn Clwyd (church of St Mary in the Clwyd Valley)

Stage 5
Graigfechan (little rock)
Moel y Gelli (bare hill of the grove)
Tyddyn tlodion (poor small farm or holding)
Llandegla (church of St. Tegla)
Pen-y-Bryn (top of the hill)
Pistyll Gwyn (white spring)
Maeshafn (field or plain of the gorge)
Afon Alun (River Alun)

Stage 6
Coed y Fedw (birch wood)
Glan Alun (Alyn river bank or hillock)
Cilcain (fine, fair, beautiful retreat or recess)
Tan-y-rhiw (under or beneath the slope)
Coed Du (black or dark wood)
Pen y Cefn (top or end of the ridge)
Garreg Boeth (hot or burnt stone or rock)
Coed Du (black or dark wood)
Hendre (winter dwelling, old home or permanent abode)
Felin Newydd (new mill)
Coed y Felin (wood of the mill)
Moel y Parc (bare hill of the park, field or enclosure)
Pant-y-pwll-dŵr (hollow or valley of the water pool or pit)

Stage 7
Brynffordd/Brynford (road of the hill)
Gorsedd (tumulus, barrow or hillock)
Lloc (a fold)
Coed y Garreg (wood of the stone or rock)
Ffordd y Ffynnon (Well Lane)

Appendix 2: SSSIs, SACs and Nature Reserves

These protected spaces are listed below in the order in which they are encountered. For detailed information on each refer to their websites.

Sites of Special Scientific Investigation (SSSIs) and Special Areas of Conservation (SACs)

Stage 1
Pen y Gogarth/Great Orme's Head SAC and SSSI
Creigiau Rhiwledyn/Little Orme's Head SSSI
Creuddyn Peninsula Woods Special Area of Conservation and the Creuddyn SSSI
Bryn Euryn SSSI

Stage 2
Mynydd Marian SSSI
Llanddulas Limestone and Gwrych Castle Wood SSSI
Coed y Gopa SSSI

Stage 3
Coedydd Ac Ogofâu Elwy A Meirchion/Lower Elwy and Meirchion Woods and Caves SSSI

Stage 4
Coed Nant Mawr SSSI

Stage 5
Graig, Llanarmon-yn-Iâl SSSI
Bryn Alyn SSSI

Stage 6
Alyn Valley Woods and Alyn Gorge Caves SSSI
Pen y Cefn Pasture SSSI
Halkyn Mountain/Mynydd Helygain SAC
Comin Helygain a GlaswellTiroedd Treffynnon/Halkyn Common and Holywell Grasslands SSSI

Stage 7
GlaswellTiroedd Trelogan/Trelogan Grasslands SSSI
Moel Hiraddug a Bryn Gop/Moel Hiraddug and Bryn Gop SSSI
Prestatyn Hillside SSSI

The North Wales Limestone Way

Nature reserves

Stage 1
North Wales Wildlife Trust Rhiwledyn Reserve
North Wales Wildlife Trust Bryn Pydew Nature Reserve
Conwy County Borough Council Bryn Euryn Local Nature Reserve

Stage 2
Conwy County Borough Council Mynydd Marian Local Nature Reserve
Coed y Gopa/Gopa Wood, managed by Coed Cadw/the Woodland Trust

Stage 5
North Wales Wildlife Trust's Graig Wyllt Nature Reserve

Stage 6
North Wales Wildlife Trust's Aberduna Nature Reserve
Denbighshire County Council Loggerheads Country Park
North Wales Wildlife Trust Coed y Felin

Appendix 3: Further Reading

For a general reference, *The Geology of Britain – an introduction* by Peter Toghill, first published in 2000 by Swan Hill Press, is recommended.

More specific to Wales, with section 5 covering the area of the walk, is *The Rocks of Wales – their story* by Dyfed Elis-Gruffydd, published by Gwasg Carreg Gwalch, 2019.

On a more technical level, focussing on petroleum geology, is a paper by Juerges et al, 2015, "The control of basin evolution on patterns of sedimentation and diagenesis: an example from the Mississippian Great Orme, North Wales" published online by the Journal of the Geological Society.

The Archaeology of Clwyd edited by John Manley, published 1991 by Gwasanaeth Archaeoleg Clwyd/Clwyd Archaeology Service, although thirty years old, provides a wealth of detail on the area of the walk.

For a fuller treatment of Welsh place names consult *Welsh Place Names Explained*, edited by Myrddin ap Dafydd, published by Gwasg Carreg Gwalch, 2016.

COMPACT CYMRU
– MORE TITLES:

www.carreg-gwalch.cymru

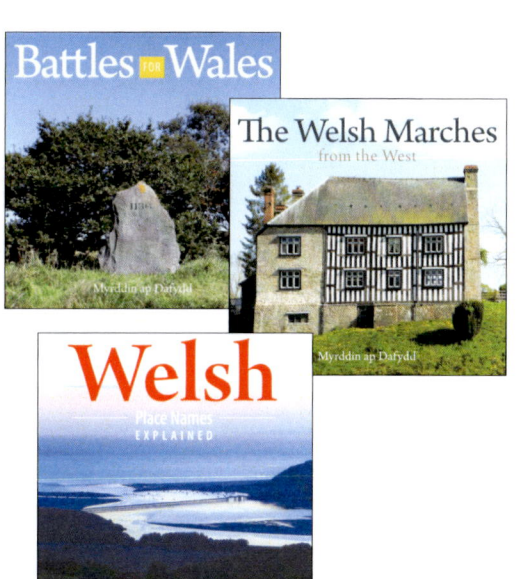

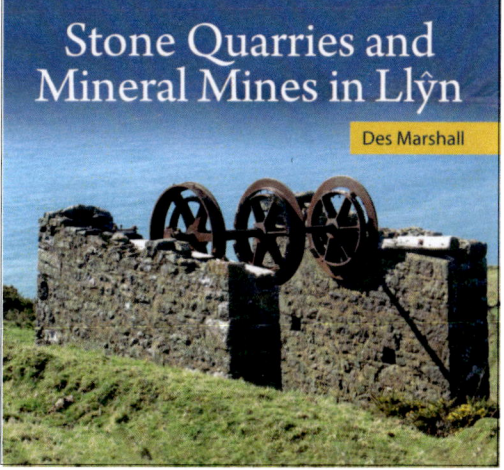

Jean Napier
Rhinogydd
Ancient Routes and Old Roads

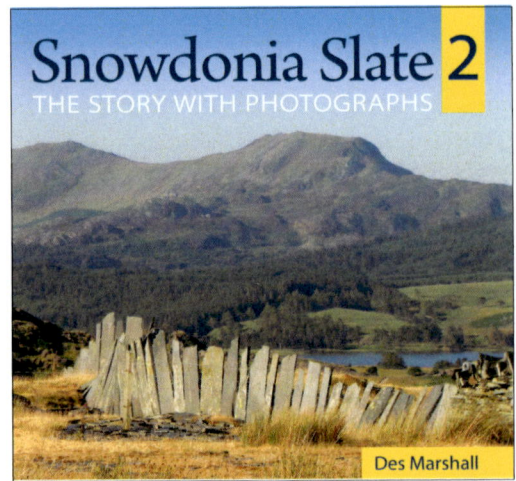

Snowdonia Slate 2
THE STORY WITH PHOTOGRAPHS

Des Marshall

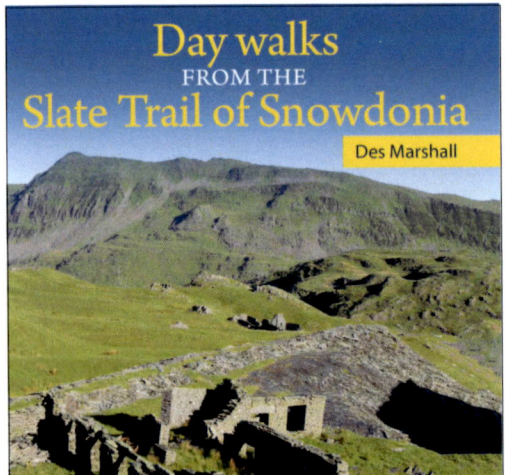

Day walks
FROM THE
Slate Trail of Snowdonia

Des Marshall

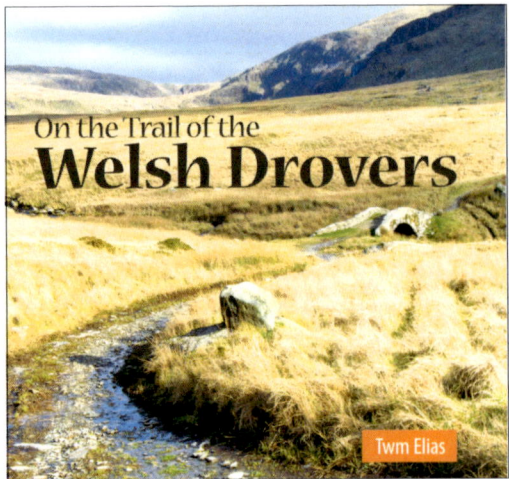

On the Trail of the
Welsh Drovers

Twm Elias